I0605414

MEN'S
2026
SOCCER
LEGENDS

PUBLISHED IN THE USA 2025 BY WELBECK CHILDREN'S BOOKS
An imprint of Hachette Children's Group
Part of Hodder & Stoughton Limited
Carmelite House, 50 Victoria Embankment, London, EC4Y 0DZ
An Hachette UK Company
www.hachette.co.uk
www.hachettechildrens.co.uk

FSC
www.fsc.org
MIX
Paper | Supporting responsible forestry
FSC® C104740

All statistical data and player heat maps provided by Opta, under license from Stats Perform.

DISCLAIMER

A catalogue record is available for this book from the British Library.

10 9 8 7 6 5 4 3 2 1
ISBN 978 1 80453 796 1

Printed and bound in Canada
Author: David Ballheimer
Senior Commissioning Editor: Suhel Ahmed
Design Manager: Matt Drew
Picture research: Paul Langan
Production: Melanie Robertson

PICTURE CREDITS
The publishers would like to thank the following sources for their kind permission to reproduce the pictures in this book.

ALAMY STOCK PHOTO: UPI 33
GETTY IMAGES: AC Milan 52; Robin Alam/ISI Photos 47; Ion Alcoba/Quality Sport Images 56; Eric Alonso/UEFA 9; Emilio Andreoli 20; ANP 37, 55, 72; Franco Arland/UEFA 35; Matias Baglietto/NurPhoto 46; Lars Baron 57; Robbie Jay Barratt/AMA 67, 98; James Baylis/AMA 109T; Giuseppe Bellini 17; Berengui/DeFodi Images 8; John Berry 21, 88; Bagu Blanco/Pressinphoto/Icon Sport 10; Mark Blinch 60; Stefan Brauer/DeFodi Images 106T; Megan Briggs 74; Rico Brouwer/Soccrates 13; Clive Brunskill 12; David S. Bustamante/Soccrates 22, 65, 78; Pedro Castillo/Real Madrid 34; Jean Catuffe 16, 82, 100; Tim Clayton/Corbis 39; Gareth Copley 106B; Oscar Del Pozo/AFP 111T; Sebastian El-Saqqa - firo sportphoto 18; Paul Ellis/AFP 85, 109B, 110T; Gualter Fatia 62; Jacques Feeney/Offside 77; Johnny Fidelin/Icon Sport 83; Franck Fife/AFP 27; Stu Forster 105; Stuart Franklin 90, 99; Sebastian Frej/MB Media 64; Edith Geuppert/GES Sportfoto 38; James Gill/Danehouse 81; GSI/Icon Sport 50; Stefano Guidi 102; Lionel Hahn 108T; Alexander Hassenstein 95; Mike Hewitt 59; Elie Hokayem/Saudi Pro League 19; Mario Hommes/DeFodi Images 49; Image Photo Agency 42, 110B; Catherine Ivill 11; Fareed Kotb/Anadolu 48; Roland Krivec/DeFodi Images 31; Harry Langer/DeFodi Images 24; Alex Livesey 63, 89, 103; Stuart MacFarlane/Arsenal FC 54, 107T; Angel Martinez 26, 61; Stefan Matzke – sampics 43; Wagner Meier 29; Doug Murray/Icon Sportswire 28; Rene Nijhuis/MB Media 75; Mattia Ozbot/Inter 23; Alex Pantling 40; Octavio Passos 97; Ryan Pierse 101; Andrew Powell/Liverpool FC 7; Antonio Pozo/Pressinphoto/Icon Sport 68; Pressinphoto/Icon Sport 44; Joe Prior/Visionhaus 15, 51; ProShots 111B; Quality Sport Images 14, 87, 96; Michael Regan 86, 107B; Maciej Rogowski/Eurasia Sport Images 92; Fran Santiago 70; Oli Scarff/AFP 5; Silas Schueller/DeFodi Images 69; Juan Manuel Serrano Arce 108B; Justin Setterfield 93; Alexandre Simoes/Borussia Dortmund 36; Nick Tre. Smith/Icon Sportswire 25; Boris Streubel 73, 91; Justin Tallis/AFP 53; Omar Vega 94; VI Images 80; Pedro Vilela 76; Visionhaus 41, 45, 66, 71, 79; Damjan Zibert/Soccrates 30

Every effort has been made to acknowledge correctly and contact the source and/or copyright holder of each picture; any unintentional errors or omissions will be corrected in future editions of this book.

All facts and stats correct as of July 2025

MEN'S 2026 SOCCER LEGENDS

STATS • PROFILES • TOP PLAYERS

WELBECK
CHILDREN'S BOOKS

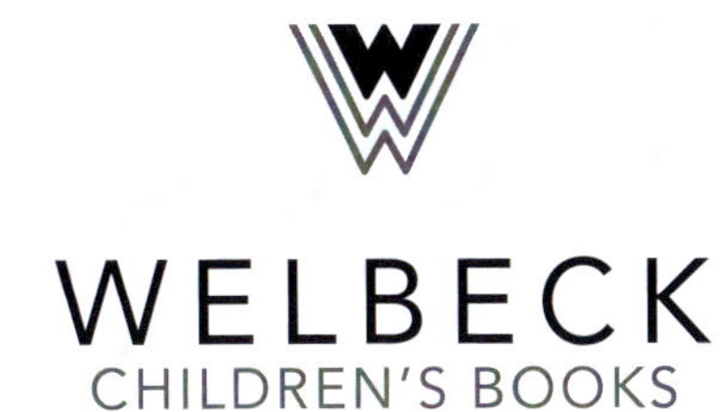

CONTENTS

HOW TO USE THIS BOOK

Welcome to *Men's Soccer Legends 2026*—the exciting book packed with the performance stats of the biggest stars in the world of soccer today! We have chosen more than 100 players and managers who are (or have been) superstars in the world's top five leagues: the Bundesliga in Germany, La Liga in Spain, France's Ligue 1, the Italian Serie A, and the English Premier League. The players are either playing in or have spent the majority of their careers up until the 2024/'25 season operating in these top leagues.

We feature exclusive performance data of today's finest defenders, midfielders, forwards, goalkeepers, and managers—data that can be compared to assess their impact in matches.

The types of stats featured for each position vary, because each position performs a specific role on the field. For example, a defender's main job is to stop the opposition from scoring, so the stats focus mainly on this part of that player's game. Likewise, a striker's tackling is not as relevant as the player's goal or assists totals. What you will find for all the players is the heat map, which shows the areas of the field the player focuses his play in or, with goalkeepers, whether their strengths lie in the six-yard box or playing as sweeper keepers, who are comfortable all around the penalty area.

The stats span a player's career to date, playing, in particular, for teams belonging to one of the top five European leagues. The figures have been collected from domestic league and European match appearances only, and exclude data from domestic cup, super cups, or international games. This narrow data pool means that the information is instantly comparable so you can decide for yourself who truly deserves to be known as a living legend of the beautiful game.

DEFENDERS

A defender's primary role is to prevent the opposing team from scoring by protecting his own goal. There are many different types of defenders (and defensive formations too) and their positions demand different skills. Full-backs play out wide and are quick and agile; they try to stop wingers and wide midfielders from delivering crosses into the penalty area. Center-backs are in the middle; they are often strong and tall so they can win the ball from dangerous forwards. Wing-backs are like full-backs, but they play in a more forward role and also attack like wingers. Teams sometimes use a spare defender called a "sweeper" who plays behind the center-backs and offers extra protection.

WHAT DO THESE STATS MEAN?

AERIAL DUELS WON

This is the percentage of headers a defender has won in his own penalty area, to interrupt an opposition attack.

INTERCEPTIONS

This is the number of times a defender has successfully stopped an attack without needing to make a tackle.

BLOCKS

A shot that is intercepted by a defender—preventing his keeper from having to make a save—counts as a block.

KEY PASSES/PASS COMPLETION

A key pass is one that results in an attacking opportunity. Pass completion indicates as a percentage the player's passing accuracy.

CLEARANCES

An attack successfully foiled, either by kicking or heading the ball away from danger, counts as a clearance.

TACKLES

This is the number of times a defender has challenged and dispossessed the opposition without committing a foul.

Did you know?

The last defender to win the Ballon d'Or, or the FIFA World's Best Player award, was Italy's Fabio Cannavaro in 2006. Only Virgil van Dijk in 2019 was voted in the top three players since 2010.

DAVID ALABA

Although his best position is left-back, David Alaba's strength is his versatility. Superb with his positioning and reading of the game, his pace and athleticism also allow him to break up attacks quickly and put his team onto the front foot.

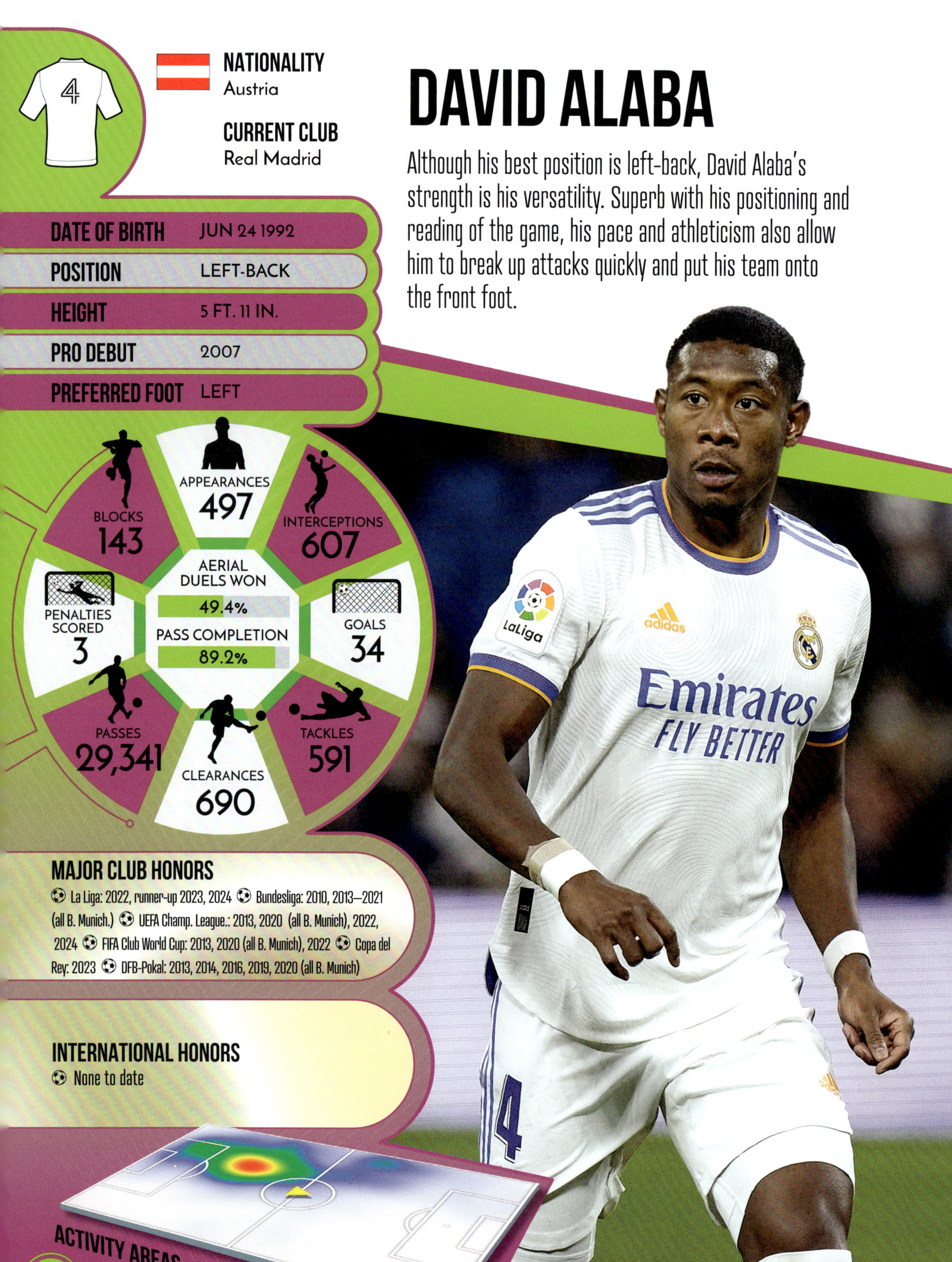

MAJOR CLUB HONORS

⚽ La Liga: 2022, runner-up 2023, 2024 ⚽ Bundesliga: 2010, 2013–2021 (all B. Munich.) ⚽ UEFA Champ. League.: 2013, 2020 (all B. Munich), 2022, 2024 ⚽ FIFA Club World Cup: 2013, 2020 (all B. Munich), 2022 ⚽ Copa del Rey: 2023 ⚽ DFB-Pokal: 2013, 2014, 2016, 2019, 2020 (all B. Munich)

INTERNATIONAL HONORS

⚽ None to date

TRENT ALEXANDER-ARNOLD

NATIONALITY
England

CURRENT CLUB
Real Madrid

Counted among the world's best overlapping defenders, Trent Alexander-Arnold plays at right-back or right wing-back. He is fast, tackles superbly, and is capable of whipping in accurate crosses that strikers love to feast on! In 2025, he moved to Real Madrid, leaving Liverpool—his boyhood club—after nine years.

DATE OF BIRTH	OCT 7 1998
POSITION	FULL-BACK
HEIGHT	5 FT. 9 IN.
PRO DEBUT	2016
PREFERRED FOOT	RIGHT

APPEARANCES 325

INTERCEPTIONS 396

GOALS 20

TACKLES 549

CLEARANCES 457

PASSES 19,125

PENALTIES SCORED 0

BLOCKS 46

AERIAL DUELS WON 37.8%

PASS COMPLETION 77.9%

MAJOR CLUB HONORS

⚽ Premier League: 2020, 2025 (all Liverpool) ⚽ UEFA Champions League: 2019 (Liverpool) ⚽ UEFA Champions League: runner-up 2018, runner-up 2022 (all Liverpool) ⚽ FIFA Club World Cup: 2019 (Liverpool) ⚽ FA Cup 2022 (Liverpool)

INTERNATIONAL HONORS

⚽ UEFA Nations League: third place 2019
⚽ UEFA European Championship: runner-up 2024

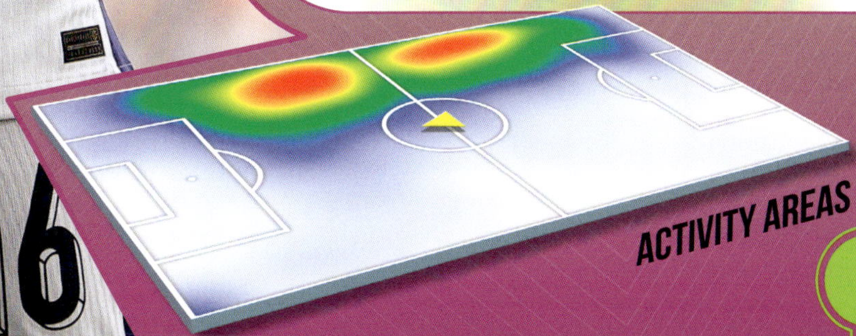

ACTIVITY AREAS

NATIONALITY
Spain

CURRENT CLUB
TBC

CÉSAR AZPILICUETA

Right-back César Azpilicueta is a natural leader, who can play anywhere on the field. He is excellent at using his positional sense to snuff out danger and frequently starts counterattacks with a great right foot. At the end of the 2024/25 season, he left Atlético Madrid after two years.

DATE OF BIRTH	AUG 28, 1989
POSITION	FULL-BACK
HEIGHT	5 FT. 10 IN.
PRO DEBUT	2006
PREFERRED FOOT	RIGHT

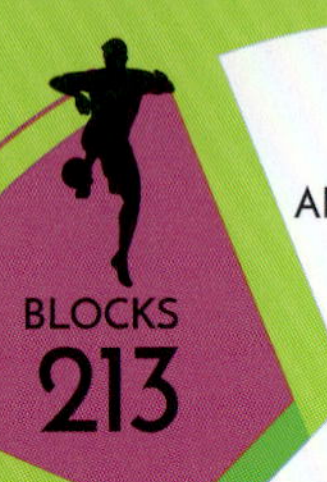

APPEARANCES 636

BLOCKS 213

INTERCEPTIONS 1,109

AERIAL DUELS WON 57.3%

PASS COMPLETION 82.1%

PENALTIES SCORED 0

GOALS 16

PASSES 31,105

TACKLES 1,606

CLEARANCES 1,911

MAJOR CLUB HONORS

⚽ Premier League: 2015, 2017 (all Chelsea) ⚽ UEFA Champions League: 2021 (Chelsea) ⚽ UEFA Europa League: 2013, 2019 (all Chelsea) ⚽ FIFA Club World Cup: 2021, runner-up 2012 (all Chelsea) ⚽ FA Cup: 2018 (Chelsea)

INTERNATIONAL HONORS

⚽ UEFA Nations League: runner-up 2021
⚽ FIFA Confederations Cup: runner-up 2013

ACTIVITY AREAS

RÚBEN DIAS

Although right-footed, Rúben Dias plays mainly on the left side of central defense, but is comfortable anywhere along the back line. He excels at winning challenges in the air and on the ground, making interceptions and delivering great passes over short and long distances with both feet.

NATIONALITY
Portugal

CURRENT CLUB
Manchester City

DATE OF BIRTH	MAY 14, 1997
POSITION	CENTRAL
HEIGHT	6 FT. 2 IN.
PRO DEBUT	2015
PREFERRED FOOT	RIGHT

APPEARANCES 212
INTERCEPTIONS 191
GOALS 6
TACKLES 230
CLEARANCES 539
PASSES 16,737
PENALTIES SCORED 0
BLOCKS 122

AERIAL DUELS WON 57.3%
PASS COMPLETION 93%

MAJOR CLUB HONORS

- Premier League: 2021, 2022, 2023, 2024
- UEFA Champions League: runner-up 2021, 2023
- Portuguese Premier Liga: 2019 (Benfica)
- FA Cup: 2023, runner-up 2025

INTERNATIONAL HONORS

- UEFA Nations League: 2019

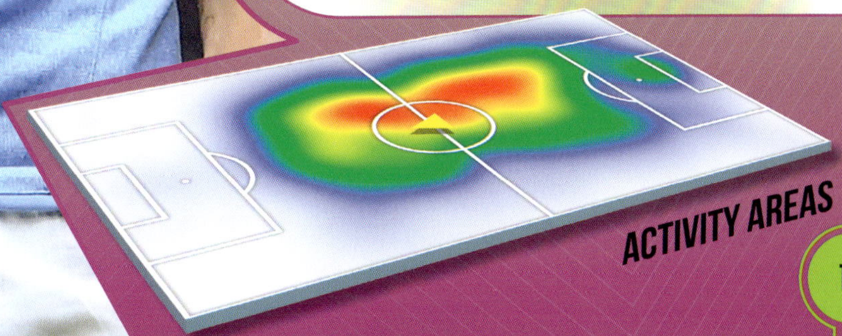

ACTIVITY AREAS

NATIONALITY
Netherlands

CURRENT CLUB
Liverpool

VIRGIL VAN DIJK

Regarded as one of the best central defenders of his generation, Virgil van Dijk's is a calm presence on the field which makes him a great leader. He has great positional sense and frequently breaks up attacks. He can also get on to the end of set pieces, making him dangerous in the opposition box.

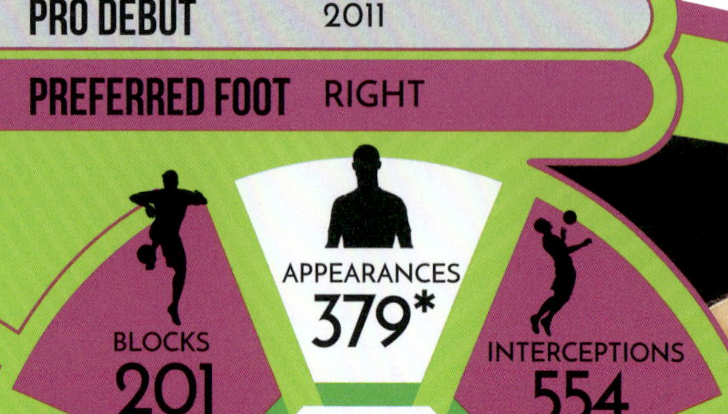

DATE OF BIRTH	JUL 08, 1991
POSITION	CENTRAL
HEIGHT	6 FT. 5 IN.
PRO DEBUT	2011
PREFERRED FOOT	RIGHT

APPEARANCES 379*
INTERCEPTIONS 554
GOALS 30
TACKLES 368
CLEARANCES 1,853
PASSES 26,695
PENALTIES SCORED 0
BLOCKS 201
AERIAL DUELS WON 74.4%
PASS COMPLETION 89.1%

*Excludes data from Scottish Premiership

MAJOR CLUB HONORS

⚽ Premier League: 2020, 2025 ⚽ Scottish Premiership: 2014, 2015 (Celtic) ⚽ UEFA Champions League: 2019, runner-up 2018, runner-up 2022 ⚽ FIFA Club World Cup: 2019 ⚽ FA Cup: 2022

INTERNATIONAL HONORS

⚽ UEFA Nations League: runner-up 2019

ACTIVITY AREAS

JEREMIE FRIMPONG

NATIONALITY
Netherlands

CURRENT CLUB
Liverpool

Jeremie Frimpong is as comfortable in midfield as he is playing as a wing-back and fits perfectly in both roles. He uses his great pace and passing ability in attacking situations, but has the technical skills to perform defensive duties. In May 2025, Frimpong joined Liverpool.

DATE OF BIRTH	DEC 10, 2000
POSITION	RIGHT WING-BACK
HEIGHT	5 FT. 8 IN.
PRO DEBUT	2019
PREFERRED FOOT	RIGHT

APPEARANCES
181*

INTERCEPTIONS
74

GOALS
27

TACKLES
198

CLEARANCES
146

PASSES
4,993

PENALTIES SCORED
0

BLOCKS
15

AERIAL DUELS WON
37.8%

PASS COMPLETION
82.1%

*Excludes data from Scottish Premiership

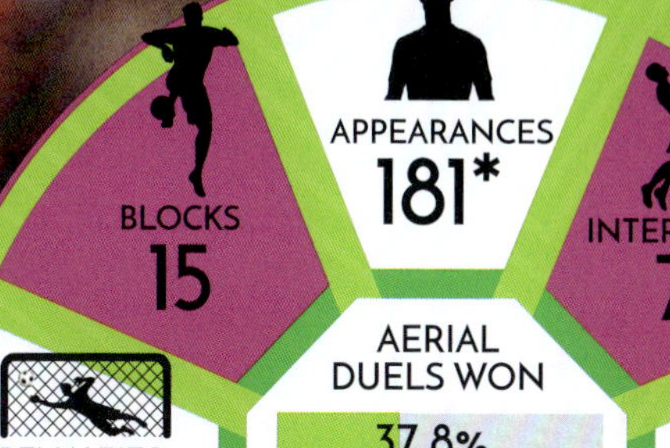

MAJOR CLUB HONORS

⚽ Bundesliga: 2024 (Bayer Leverkusen) ⚽ UEFA Europa League: runner-up 2024 (Bayer Leverkusen) ⚽ DFB-Pokal 2024 (Bayer Leverkusen) ⚽ Scottish Premiership: 2020 (Celtic) ⚽ Scottish Cup: 2020 (Celtic)

INTERNATIONAL HONORS

⚽ UEFA Nations League: runner-up 2019

ACTIVITY AREAS

NATIONALITY
Uruguay

CURRENT CLUB
Atlético Madrid

JOSÉ GIMÉNEZ

The Uruguayan is a tough-tackling center-back who is quick off the mark and difficult to knock off the ball. He made his international debut when he was just 19 and has also thrived at club level since joining Atlético Madrid in 2013.

DATE OF BIRTH	JAN 20, 1995
POSITION	CENTRAL
HEIGHT	6 FT. 1 IN.
PRO DEBUT	RIGHT
PREFERRED FOOT	

APPEARANCES 323
INTERCEPTIONS 471
GOALS 10
TACKLES 450
CLEARANCES 1,447
PASSES 12,521
PENALTIES SCORED 0
BLOCKS 196
AERIAL DUELS WON 63.6%
PASS COMPLETION 84.7%

MAJOR CLUB HONORS
- La Liga: 2014, 2021
- UEFA Europa League: 2018
- UEFA Super Cup: 2018
- UEFA Champions League: runner-up 2014, 2016

INTERNATIONAL HONORS
- FIFA U-20 World Cup: runner-up 2013
- Copa América: third place 2024

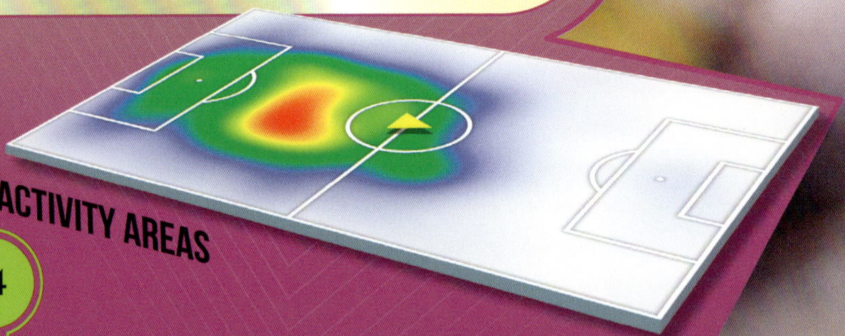

ACTIVITY AREAS

JOŠKO GVARDIOL

Joško Gvardiol is a master in one-on-one situations, knowing exactly when to block or make a tackle. He reads the game well and is clever at making interceptions. His sound technique at the back is matched by his ability to turn defense into attack.

NATIONALITY
Croatia

CURRENT CLUB
Manchester City

DATE OF BIRTH	JAN 23, 2002
POSITION	CENTRAL
HEIGHT	6 FT. 1 IN.
PRO DEBUT	2019
PREFERRED FOOT	LEFT

APPEARANCES 169
INTERCEPTIONS 216
GOALS 16
TACKLES 245
CLEARANCES 356
PASSES 11,377
PENALTIES SCORED 0
BLOCKS 76
AERIAL DUELS WON 56.1%
PASS COMPLETION 88.3%

MAJOR CLUB HONORS
⚽ Premier League: 2024 ⚽ DFB Pokal: 2022, 2023 (RP Leipzig) ⚽ UEFA Super Cup: 2023 ⚽ FIFA Club World Cup: 2023

INTERNATIONAL HONORS
⚽ FIFA World Cup: third place 2022
⚽ Copa América third place 2024

ACTIVITY AREAS

NATIONALITY
Morocco

CURRENT CLUB
Paris Saint-Germain

ACHRAF HAKIMI

Known for his versatility, Ashraf Hakimi is equally good as a right-sided wing-back as he is in midfield. His exceptional pace allows him to stop opposition attackers with clean tackles or interceptions and he can than leave opponents behind when he joins the attack.

DATE OF BIRTH	NOV 04, 1998
POSITION	RIGHT-BACK
HEIGHT	5 FT. 11 IN.
PRO DEBUT	2016
PREFERRED FOOT	RIGHT

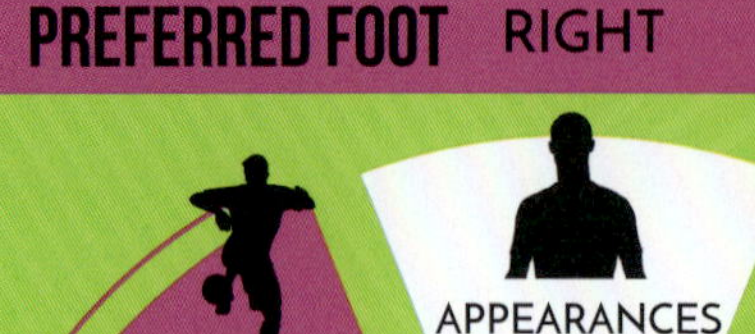

APPEARANCES 274
INTERCEPTIONS 238
GOALS 42
TACKLES 495
CLEARANCES 232
PASSES 15,499
PENALTIES SCORED 0
BLOCKS 26
AERIAL DUELS WON 41.9%
PASS COMPLETION 87.8%

MAJOR CLUB HONORS
⚽ Ligue 1: 2022, 2023, 2024, 2025 ⚽ Serie A: 2021 (Inter Milan) ⚽ UEFA Champions League: 2018 (R. Madrid), 2025 ⚽ FIFA World Club Cup: 2017, runner-up 2025, (R. Madrid) ⚽ Coupe de France: 2024, 2025

INTERNATIONAL HONORS
⚽ None to date

ACTIVITY AREAS

THEO HERNÁNDEZ

Known more for his attacking qualities than his defensive work, Theo Hernández (younger brother of Lucas) is a player who is blessed with great pace; he can dribble rapidly with the ball at his feet and get into goalscoring positions. A fan favourite at AC Milan, Hernández left the club in 2025 after five seasons.

NATIONALITY
France

CURRENT CLUB
Al Hilal (S. Arabia)

DATE OF BIRTH	OCT 06, 1997
POSITION	LEFT-BACK
HEIGHT	6 FT.
PRO DEBUT	2015
PREFERRED FOOT	LEFT

APPEARANCES 312
INTERCEPTIONS 288
GOALS 34
TACKLES 476
CLEARANCES 433
PASSES 13,597
PENALTIES SCORED 4
BLOCKS 71

AERIAL DUELS WON 65%
PASS COMPLETION 84.4%

MAJOR CLUB HONORS

⚽ Serie A: 2022 (AC Milan) ⚽ UEFA Champions League: 2018 (Real Madrid) ⚽ FIFA World Club Cup: 2017 (Real Madrid)

INTERNATIONAL HONORS

⚽ FIFA World Cup: runner-up 2022
⚽ UEFA Nations League: 2021, third place 2025

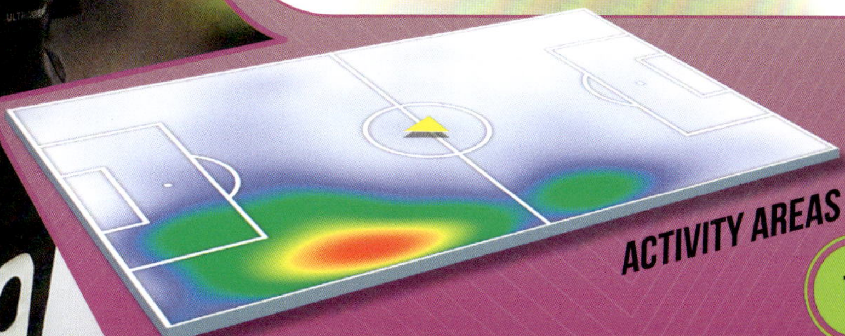

ACTIVITY AREAS

NATIONALITY
Germany

CURRENT CLUB
Bayern Munich

JOSHUA KIMMICH

A top-class player who excels at right-back, Joshua Kimmich is also adaptable and can play in most defensive and midfield positions. He is a natural leader and communicator on the field with an array of skills, including positional sense, timing, anticipation, tackling, passing, heading, and stamina.

DATE OF BIRTH	FEB 08, 1995
POSITION	RIGHT-BACK
HEIGHT	5 FT. 10 IN.
PRO DEBUT	2013
PREFERRED FOOT	RIGHT

APPEARANCES 392

INTERCEPTIONS 424

GOALS 41

TACKLES 588

CLEARANCES 339

PASSES 28,698

PENALTIES SCORED 2

BLOCKS 76

AERIAL DUELS WON 44.7%

PASS COMPLETION 90.4%

MAJOR CLUB HONORS

⚽ Bundesliga: 2016, 2017, 2018, 2019, 2020, 2021, 2022, 2023, 2025 ⚽ UEFA Champions League: 2020 ⚽ DFB-Pokal: 2016, 2019, 2020 ⚽ FIFA Club World Cup: 2020

INTERNATIONAL HONORS

⚽ FIFA Confederations Cup: 2017

ACTIVITY AREAS

AYMERIC LAPORTE

Aymeric Laporte was among Europe's best defenders before moving to the Saudi Pro League in 2023. He is a powerful tackler, excellent in the air, and a good organizer at the back. Laporte can also start attacks with his precise passing out of defense.

NATIONALITY
Spain

CURRENT CLUB
Al Nassr (S. Arabia)

DATE OF BIRTH	MAY 27, 1994
POSITION	CENTRAL
HEIGHT	6 FT. 2 IN.
PRO DEBUT	2011
PREFERRED FOOT	LEFT

APPEARANCES 392

INTERCEPTIONS 669

GOALS 25

TACKLES 599

CLEARANCES 1,334

PASSES 25,327

PENALTIES SCORED 0

BLOCKS 154

AERIAL DUELS WON 64.9%

PASS COMPLETION 88.7%

MAJOR CLUB HONORS

⚽ Premier League: 2018, 2019, 2021, 2022, 2023 (all Man. City) ⚽ UEFA Champions League: runner-up 2021, 2023 (all Man. City) ⚽ FA Cup: 2019, 2023 (all Man. City)

INTERNATIONAL HONORS

⚽ UEFA Nations League: runner-up 2021, 2023
⚽ UEFA European Championship: 2024

ACTIVITY AREAS

GIOVANNI DI LORENZO

22

NATIONALITY
Italy

CURRENT CLUB
Napoli

Although he began his professional career as an attacking player, Giovanni di Lorenzo is now an excellent defender, normally positioned at right-back, but he can play in the middle too. He has a solid tackling technique, is physically strong, and possesses good aerial ability.

DATE OF BIRTH	AUG 04, 1993
POSITION	RIGHT-BACK
HEIGHT	6 FT.
PRO DEBUT	2010
PREFERRED FOOT	BOTH

APPEARANCES 291

INTERCEPTIONS 253

GOALS 22

TACKLES 527

CLEARANCES 433

PASSES 16,478

PENALTIES SCORED 0

BLOCKS 85

AERIAL DUELS WON 52.5%

PASS COMPLETION 85.9%

MAJOR CLUB HONORS

- Serie A: 2023, 2025
- Coppa Italia: 2020

INTERNATIONAL HONORS

- UEFA European Championship: 2020 (2021)
- UEFA Nations League: third place 2021, 2023

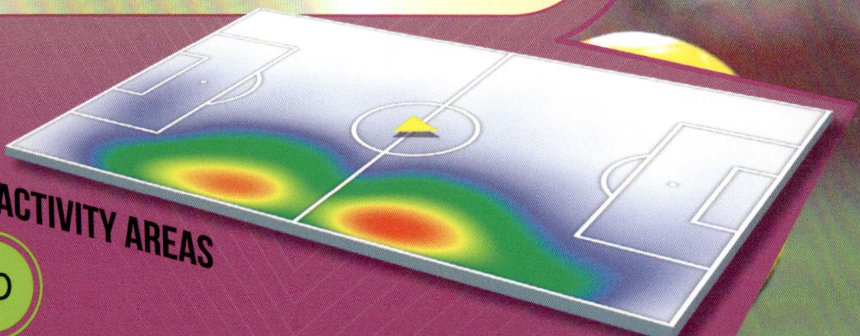

ACTIVITY AREAS

MARQUINHOS

Marquinhos is a smart defender. He may not be a powerhouse like many of today's top-class center-backs, but has the speed, agility, and intelligence to mark the quickest forwards, plus he can be very effective going forward.

NATIONALITY
Brazil

CURRENT CLUB
Paris Saint-Germain

DATE OF BIRTH	MAY 14, 1994
POSITION	CENTRAL
HEIGHT	6 FT.
PRO DEBUT	2012
PREFERRED FOOT	RIGHT

APPEARANCES	451
INTERCEPTIONS	568
GOALS	35
TACKLES	681
CLEARANCES	1,554
PASSES	29,098
PENALTIES SCORED	0
BLOCKS	290
AERIAL DUELS WON	57.8%
PASS COMPLETION	92.8%

MAJOR CLUB HONORS

⚽ Ligue 1: 2014, 2015, 2016, 2018, 2019, 2020, 2022, 2023, 2024, 2025 ⚽ UEFA Champions League: runner-up 2020, 2025 ⚽ FIFA World Club Cup: runner-up 2025 ⚽ Coupe de France: 2015, 2016, 2017, 2018, runner-up 2019, 2020, 2021, 2024, 2025

INTERNATIONAL HONORS

⚽ Copa América: 2019, runner-up 2021
⚽ Olympic Games: 2016

ACTIVITY AREAS

NATIONALITY
Argentina

CURRENT CLUB
Atlético Madrid

NAHUEL MOLINA

Nahuel Molina has worked hard to become a dominant force on the right flank. Very quick, with fine positional sense and good tackling technique, he is also comfortable with the ball at his feet and a tremendous passer in attacking situations.

DATE OF BIRTH	APR 06, 1998
POSITION	RIGHT-BACK
HEIGHT	5 FT.9 IN.
PRO DEBUT	2016
PREFERRED FOOT	RIGHT

APPEARANCES 181
INTERCEPTIONS 97
GOALS 16
TACKLES 258
CLEARANCES 218
PASSES 6,249
PENALTIES SCORED 0
BLOCKS 24
AERIAL DUELS WON 39.4%
PASS COMPLETION 78.3%

MAJOR CLUB HONORS
- None to date

INTERNATIONAL HONORS
- FIFA World Cup: 2022
- Copa América: 2021, 2024
- CONMEBOL–UEFA Cup of Champions: 2022

ACTIVITY AREAS

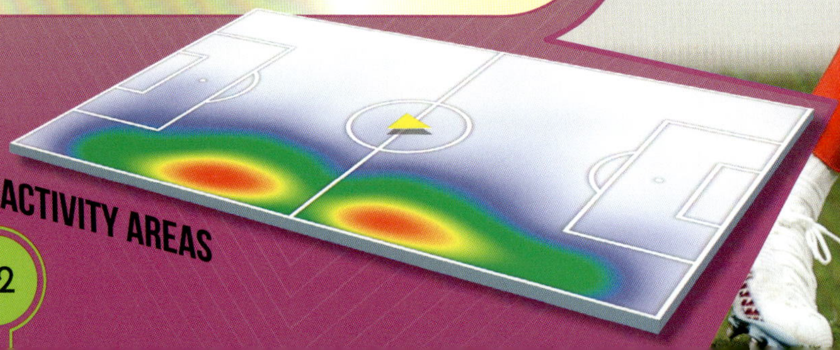

BENJAMIN PAVARD

One of the most accomplished defenders in world soccer, Benjamin Pavard has the ability to time his tackle perfectly and shut down opposing players in possession of the ball. He has genuine pace and can also move the ball down one or two lines of defense with an incisive pass.

NATIONALITY
France

CURRENT CLUB
Inter Milan

DATE OF BIRTH	MAR 28, /1996
POSITION	CENTRAL
HEIGHT	6 FT. 1 IN.
PRO DEBUT	2014
PREFERRED FOOT	RIGHT

APPEARANCES	293
INTERCEPTIONS	468
GOALS	12
TACKLES	414
CLEARANCES	860
PASSES	17,126
PENALTIES SCORED	0
BLOCKS	149
AERIAL DUELS WON	60.2%
PASS COMPLETION	88%

MAJOR CLUB HONORS

⚽ Serie A: 2024 ⚽ Bundesliga: 2020, 2021, 2022, 2023 (all B. Munich) ⚽ UEFA Champions League: 2020 (B. Munich), runner-up 2025 ⚽ FIFA Club World Cup: 2020 (B. Munich) ⚽ DFB-Pokal: 2020 (B. Munich)

INTERNATIONAL HONORS

⚽ FIFA World Cup: 2018, runner-up 2022
⚽ UEFA Nations League: 2021, third place 2025

ACTIVITY AREAS

NATIONALITY
Scotland

CURRENT CLUB
Liverpool

ANDREW ROBERTSON

Andrew Robertson has become one of the world's most reliable defenders, carrying out his duties without fuss or flashiness. Aside from his defensive skill set, he has the ability to hare down the flank, complete neat one-twos, and whip over dangerous crosses, which make him an asset in attack.

DATE OF BIRTH	MAR 11, 1994
POSITION	LEFT-BACK
HEIGHT	5 FT. 10 IN.
PRO DEBUT	2012
PREFERRED FOOT	LEFT

APPEARANCES 372

INTERCEPTIONS 329

GOALS 12

TACKLES 550

CLEARANCES 627

PASSES 21,032

PENALTIES SCORED 0

BLOCKS 69

AERIAL DUELS WON 50.4%

PASS COMPLETION 84.1%

MAJOR CLUB HONORS

⚽ Premier League: 2020, 2025 ⚽ UEFA Champions League: 2019 ⚽ FIFA World Club Cup: 2019 ⚽ UEFA Super Cup: 2019 ⚽ FA Cup: 2022

INTERNATIONAL HONORS

⚽ None to date

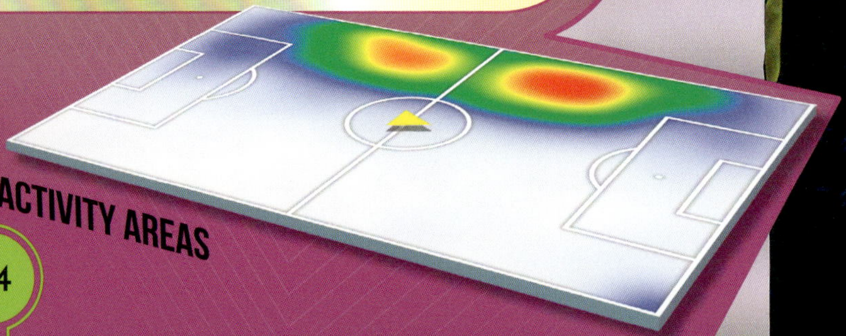

ACTIVITY AREAS

ANTONEE ROBINSON

An energetic and dynamic presence on the field, Antonee Robinson is a solid tackler and he reads the game well, consistently making timely interceptions. He has natural pace, too, and is a willing attacker, making overlapping runs and joining in attacks in the final third.

NATIONALITY
USA

CURRENT CLUB
Fulham

DATE OF BIRTH	AUG 08, 1997
POSITION	LEFT-BACK
HEIGHT	6 FT.
PRO DEBUT	2015
PREFERRED FOOT	LEFT

APPEARANCES 136

INTERCEPTIONS 232

GOALS 0

TACKLES 295

CLEARANCES 362

PASSES 5,770

PENALTIES SCORED 0

BLOCKS 31

AERIAL DUELS WON 62.7%

PASS COMPLETION 77.4%

MAJOR CLUB HONORS

- EFL Championship: 2022

INTERNATIONAL HONORS

- CONCACAF Nations League: 2020, 2023, 2024

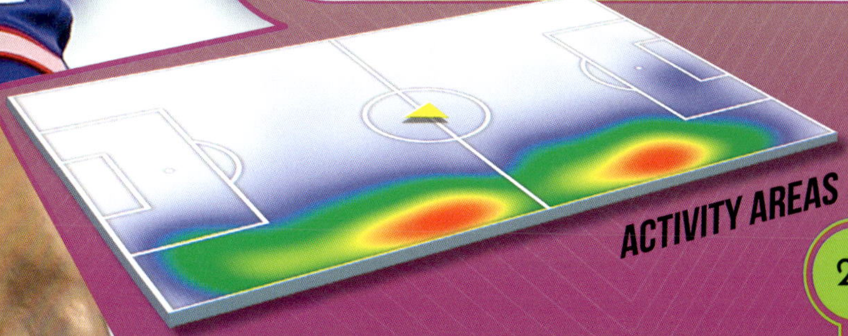

ACTIVITY AREAS

NATIONALITY
Germany

CURRENT CLUB
Real Madrid

ANTONIO RÜDIGER

Antonio Rüdiger is a dominant defender all along the back line, winning tackles with his strength and taking charge of the penalty area with his heading ability. He is also an excellent passer, reads the game well, and leads by example.

DATE OF BIRTH	03 MAR, 1993
POSITION	CENTRAL
HEIGHT	6 FT. 3 IN.
PRO DEBUT	2011
PREFERRED FOOT	RIGHT

APPEARANCES
435

INTERCEPTIONS
394

GOALS
19

TACKLES
543

CLEARANCES
1,436

PASSES
25,407

PENALTIES SCORED
0

BLOCKS
182

AERIAL DUELS WON
59.3%

PASS COMPLETION
88.1%

MAJOR CLUB HONORS
⚽ La Liga: 2024 ⚽ UEFA Champions League: 2021 (Chelsea), 2024 ⚽ FIFA World Club Cup: 2021 (Chelsea), 2022 ⚽ UEFA Europa League 2019 (Chelsea) ⚽ UEFA Super Cup: 2021 (Chelsea), 2022, 2024 ⚽ FA Cup: 2018 (Chelsea) ⚽ Copa del Rey: 2023

INTERNATIONAL HONORS
⚽ FIFA Confederations Cup: 2017

ACTIVITY AREAS

WILLIAM SALIBA

When William Saliba was just six years old he was coached by Kylian Mbappe's father, and the central defender has followed the legendary Frenchman on to the national team. A solid tackler, he is a calm, solid presence in defense with excellent timing, plus immense positional awareness.

NATIONALITY
France

CURRENT CLUB
Arsenal

DATE OF BIRTH	MAR 24, 2001
POSITION	CENTER-BACK
HEIGHT	6 FT. 4 IN.
PRO DEBUT	2018
PREFERRED FOOT	RIGHT

APPEARANCES 224

INTERCEPTIONS 229

GOALS 8

TACKLES 303

CLEARANCES 620

PASSES 15,860

PENALTIES SCORED 0

BLOCKS 100

AERIAL DUELS WON 60.3%

PASS COMPLETION 92%

MAJOR CLUB HONORS
- Coupe de France: runner-up 2020 (PSG)

INTERNATIONAL HONORS
- FIFA World Cup: runners-up 2022

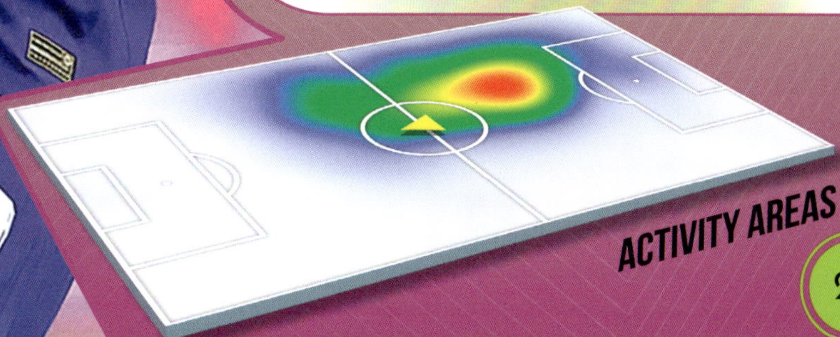

ACTIVITY AREAS

NATIONALITY
Italy

CURRENT CLUB
Atalanta

GEORGIO SCALVINI

A tall center-back who is both excellent in the air and a technically sound tackler, Georgio Scalvani came to prominence in 2024,though a bad knee injury just before the EURO championship halted his rise. He is back now and many experts believe he will grow into a world-class defender.

DATE OF BIRTH	DEC 11, 2003
POSITION	CENTER-BACK
HEIGHT	6 FT. 4 IN.
PRO DEBUT	2021
PREFERRED FOOT	RIGHT

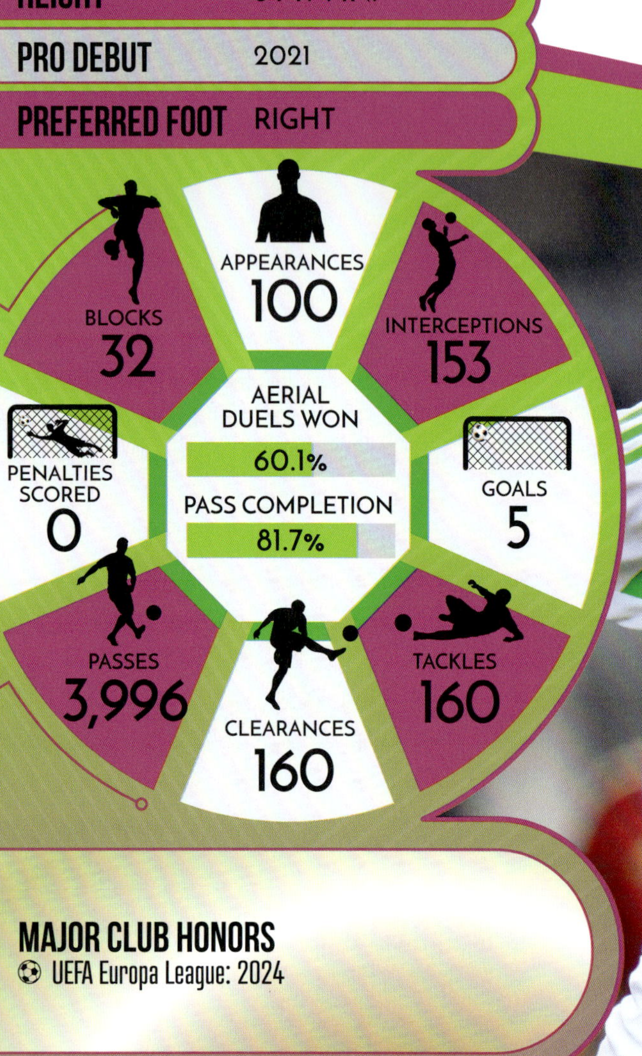

MAJOR CLUB HONORS

- UEFA Europa League: 2024

INTERNATIONAL HONORS

- None to date

ACTIVITY AREAS

THIAGO SILVA

Thiago Silva has long been recognized as one of the world's best central defenders—some experts considering him an all-time great. A leader on the field, his all-around awareness ensures he is always perfectly placed to make important interventions.

NATIONALITY
Brazil

CURRENT CLUB
Fluminense (Brazil)

DATE OF BIRTH	SEP 22, 1984
POSITION	CENTER-BACK
HEIGHT	6 FT.
PRO DEBUT	2002
PREFERRED FOOT	RIGHT

APPEARANCES 556

INTERCEPTIONS 1,064

GOALS 27

TACKLES 760

CLEARANCES 2,710

PASSES 35,769

PENALTIES SCORED 0

BLOCKS 370

AERIAL DUELS WON 71.3%

PASS COMPLETION 92.7%

MAJOR CLUB HONORS

⚽ UEFA Champions League: 2021 (Chelsea), runner-up 2020 (PSG) ⚽ UEFA Super Cup: 2021 (Chelsea) ⚽ FIFA Club World Cup: 2021 (Chelsea) ⚽ Serie A: 2011 (AC Milan) ⚽ Ligue 1: 2013-2020 (PSG) ⚽ Coupe de France: 2015-18, 2020 (all PSG) ⚽ FA Cup: 2022 (Chelsea)

INTERNATIONAL HONORS

- ⚽ FIFA Confederations Cup; 2013
- ⚽ Copa América: 2019, runner-up 2021
- ⚽ Olympic Games: silver medal 2012, bronze medal 2008

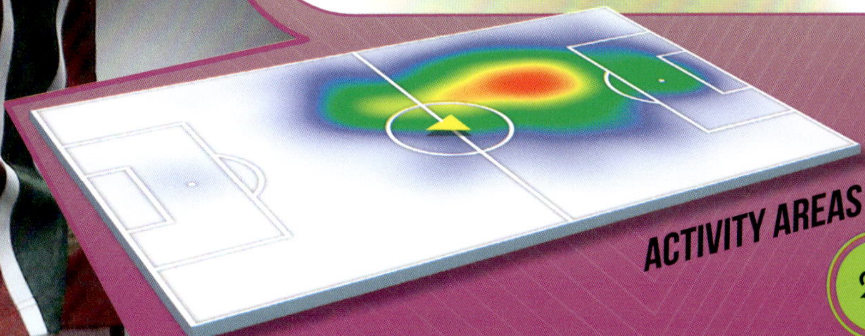

ACTIVITY AREAS

MILAN ŠKRINIAR

Center-back Milan Škriniar is a forceful tackler, strong in the air and combative on the ground. But what sets Škriniar apart are his ball-playing skills, as well as his ability to stay calm under pressure and pick out intelligent passes.

DATE OF BIRTH	FEB 11, 1995
POSITION	CENTER-BACK
HEIGHT	6 FT. 2 IN.
PRO DEBUT	2012
PREFERRED FOOT	RIGHT

MAJOR CLUB HONORS

⚽ Ligue 1: 2024, 2025 (PSG) ⚽ Serie A: 2021 (Inter Milan) ⚽ UEFA Champions League: runner-up 2023 (Inter Milan), 2025 ⚽ UEFA Europa League: runner-up 2020 (Inter Milan) ⚽ Coupe de France: 2024, 2025 (all PSG) ⚽ Coppa Italia: 2022, 2023 (Inter Milan)

INTERNATIONAL HONORS

⚽ King's Cup: 2018

DAYOT UPAMECANO

Dayot Upamecano has developed into an exceptional center-half with all the talents needed for the position. His standout talent is his ability with the ball at his feet—a quality that complements his passing accuracy.

NATIONALITY
France

CURRENT CLUB
Bayern Munich

DATE OF BIRTH	OCT 27, 1998
POSITION	CENTER-BACK
HEIGHT	6 FT. 1 IN.
PRO DEBUT	2015
PREFERRED FOOT	RIGHT

APPEARANCES	284
INTERCEPTIONS	412
GOALS	8
TACKLES	556
CLEARANCES	817
PASSES	19,724
PENALTIES SCORED	0
BLOCKS	102
AERIAL DUELS WON	60.6%
PASS COMPLETION	89.2%

MAJOR CLUB HONORS

- Bundesliga: 2022, 2023, 2025
- DFL Supercup: 2021

INTERNATIONAL HONORS

- UEFA Nations League: 2021
- FIFA World Cup: runner-up 2022

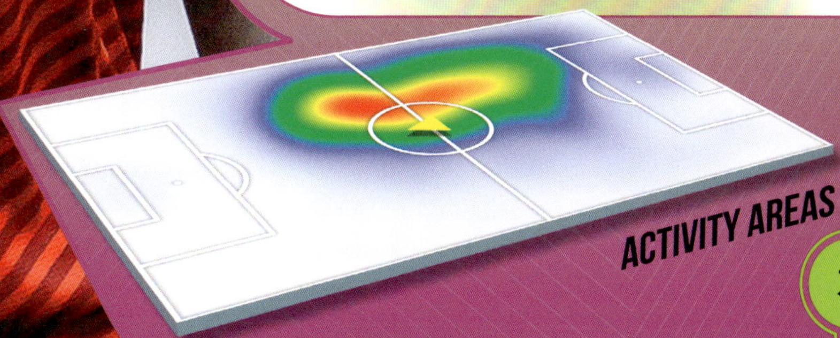

ACTIVITY AREAS

MIDFIELDERS

Midfielders are the heartbeat of a team. Not only do they play between the forwards and the defenders, but they also help out their teammates at both ends. Midfielders fall into one of four main categories: 1) defensive midfielders, who sit in front of the back four and are great tacklers; 2) the attacking full-backs operating on the wings, who whip crosses into the box; 3) the central midfielders, who are brilliant at setting up and then joining attacks, as well as helping out in defense whenever needed; 4) the playmakers—these are the stars who build the attack with their creative play.

WHAT DO THE STATS MEAN?

ASSISTS

A pass, cross, or header to a team-mate who then scores counts as an assist. This stat also includes a deflected shot that is converted by a teammate.

SHOTS

Any deliberate strike on goal counts as a shot. The strike does not have to be on target or force a save from the keeper.

CHANCES CREATED

Any pass that results in a shot at goal (whether or not the goal is scored) is regarded as a chance created.

TACKLES

This is the number of times the player has challenged and dispossessed the opposition without committing a foul.

DRIBBLES

This is the number of times the player has gone past an opponent while running with the ball.

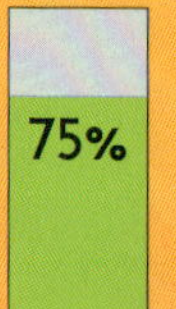

SUCCESSFUL PASSES

This shows as a percentage how successful the midfielder is at finding team-mates with passes, whether over 5 or 60 yards.

Did you know?

Midfielders tend to do the most running in a game. "Box to box" central midfielders will cover between 6 and 7.5 miles (more than a quarter of a marathon) over 90 minutes.

NATIONALITY
England

CURRENT CLUB
Real Madrid

JUDE BELLINGHAM

Jude Bellingham's talent was evident when he was just 16 years old! Now he has fulfilled that promise and become one of the world's best midfielders playing for one of the world's best clubs. He is a good tackler, exceptionally quick, positionally aware, and able to create and score goals.

DATE OF BIRTH	JUN 29, 2003
POSITION	CENTRAL
HEIGHT	6 FT. 1 IN.
PRO DEBUT	2019
PREFERRED FOOT	RIGHT

APPEARANCES
201

ASSISTS
44

DRIBBLES
600

PASSES
9,408

SUCCESSFUL PASSES
86.1%

PENALTIES SCORED
3

GOALS
55

SHOTS
354

CHANCES CREATED
252

TACKLES
387

MAJOR CLUB HONORS

- La Liga: 2024
- UEFA Champions League: 2024
- Bundesliga: runner-up 2023 (Borussia Dortmund)
- DFB-Pokal: 2021 (Borussia Dortmund)

INTERNATIONAL HONORS

- UEFA European Championship: runner-up 2020 (2021), runner-up 2024

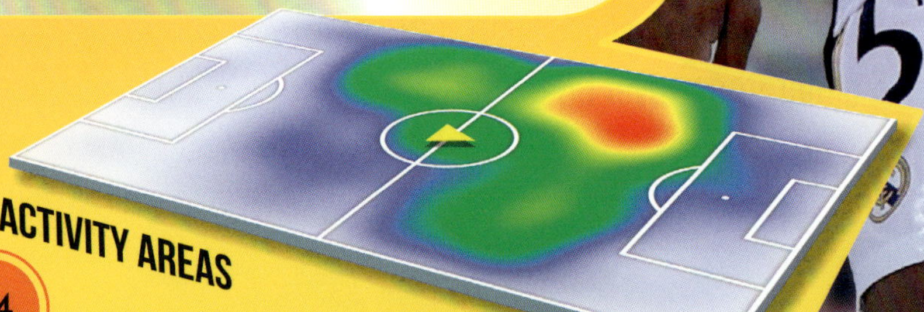

ACTIVITY AREAS

KEVIN DE BRUYNE

Kevin De Bruyne ranks as one of the finest attacking midfielders of his generation. Strong and technically brilliant, he can break up play at one end and almost immediately blast a 25-yard shot into the opposite goal. In 2025, he joined Napoli after a decade at Man City.

NATIONALITY
Belgium

CURRENT CLUB
Napoli

DATE OF BIRTH	JUN 28, 1991
POSITION	ATTACKING
HEIGHT	5 FT. 11 IN.
PRO DEBUT	2008
PREFERRED FOOT	RIGHT

ASSISTS
184

APPEARANCES
463

DRIBBLES
1,287

PENALTIES SCORED
5

PASSES
21,863

SUCCESSFUL PASSES
80.7%

GOALS
116

SHOTS
1,105

CHANCES CREATED
1,314

TACKLES
531

MAJOR CLUB HONORS

- Premier League: 2018, 2019, 2021, 2022, 2023, 2024 (all Man City)
- UEFA Champions League: runner-up 2021, 2023 (all Man City)
- FA Cup: 2019, 2023 (all Man City)
- DFB-Pokal: 2015 (VfL Wolfsburg)

INTERNATIONAL HONORS

- FIFA World Cup: third place 2018

ACTIVITY AREAS

EMRE CAN

Having been a defender earlier in his career, Emre Can has grown into a classy central midfielder. He combines his excellent tackling strength with his midfielder's instincts to thread passes to teammates in attacking positions.

DATE OF BIRTH	JAN 12, 1994
POSITION	CENTRAL
HEIGHT	6 FT. 1 IN.
PRO DEBUT	2011
PREFERRED FOOT	RIGHT

MAJOR CLUB HONORS

⚽ Bundesliga: 2013 (B. Munich), runner-up 2023 ⚽ UEFA Champions League: 2013 (B. Munich), runner-up 2018 (Liverpool), runner-up 2024 ⚽ UEFA Europa League: runner-up 2016 (Liverpool) ⚽ Serie A: 2019, 2020 (Juventus) ⚽ DFB-Pokal: 2013 (B. Munich) 2021

INTERNATIONAL HONORS

⚽ FIFA Confederations Cup: 2017

EDUARDO CAMAVINGA

Eduardo Camavinga is outstanding as a defensive midfielder and also very effective at left-back. He reads the game extremely well, making timely interceptions and strong tackles and launching incisive attacks with his accurate passing. He has great stamina too.

NATIONALITY
France

CURRENT CLUB
Real Madrid

DATE OF BIRTH	NOV 10, 2002
POSITION	DEFENSIVE
HEIGHT	6 FT. 1 IN.
PRO DEBUT	2019
PREFERRED FOOT	LEFT

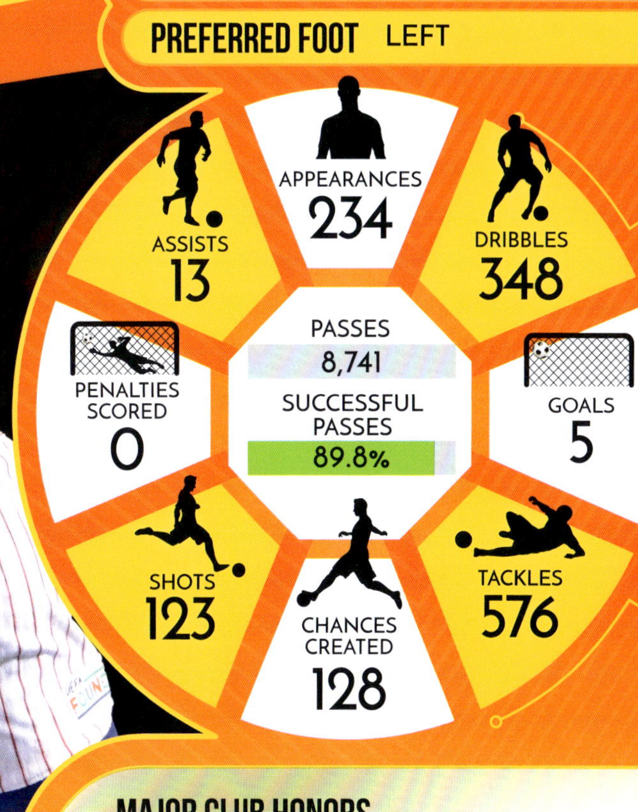

MAJOR CLUB HONORS

⚽ La Liga: 2022, 2024 ⚽ UEFA Champions League: 2022, 2024 ⚽ Copa del Rey: 2023 ⚽ FIFA Club World Cup: 2022 ⚽ FIFA Intercontinental Cup: 2024

INTERNATIONAL HONORS

⚽ FIFA World Cup: runner-up 2022

ACTIVITY AREAS

ALPHONSO DAVIES

Ghana-born Alphonso Davies is already considered one of the finest male soccer players to represent Canada. He can confidentally deliver in all left-sided positions thanks to his pace, dribbling talent, passing creativity, stamina, and crossing ability.

19

NATIONALITY
Canada

CURRENT CLUB
Bayern Munich

DATE OF BIRTH	NOV 02, 2000
POSITION	LEFT WING
HEIGHT	6 FT.
PRO DEBUT	2016
PREFERRED FOOT	LEFT

APPEARANCES 270

DRIBBLES 1,226

GOALS 20

TACKLES 463

CHANCES CREATED 306

SHOTS 180

PENALTIES SCORED 0

ASSISTS 38

PASSES 11,332

SUCCESSFUL PASSES 86.9%

MAJOR CLUB HONORS

⚽ Bundesliga: 2019, 2020, 2021, 2022, 2023, 2025 ⚽ UEFA Champions League: 2020 ⚽ FIFA Club World Cup 2020 ⚽ UEFA Super Cup: 2020 ⚽ DFB-Pokal: 2019, 2020

INTERNATIONAL HONORS

⚽ None to date

ACTIVITY AREAS

OUSMANE DEMBÉLÉ

Ousmane Dembélé's speed, dribbling skills, and ability to take on defenders make him a natural winger. Capable of playing on either flank, he frequently uses his pace and technical skills to create goal-scoring opportunities for himself or provide key passes and assists to his teammates.

NATIONALITY
France

CURRENT CLUB
Paris Saint-Germain

DATE OF BIRTH	MAY 15, 1997
POSITION	WINGER
HEIGHT	5 FT. 10 IN.
PRO DEBUT	2014
PREFERRED FOOT	BOTH

APPEARANCES 312

ASSISTS 83

DRIBBLES 1,498

PENALTIES SCORED 3

PASSES 9,507

SUCCESSFUL PASSES 80%

GOALS 86

SHOTS 650

CHANCES CREATED 565

TACKLES 226

MAJOR CLUB HONORS

⚽ Ligue 1: 2024, 2025 ⚽ UEFA Champions League: 2025 ⚽ La Liga: 2018, 2019, 2023 (all Barcelona) ⚽ Coupe de France: 2024, 2025 ⚽ FIFA World Club Cup: runner-up 2025 ⚽ Copa del Rey: 2018, 2021 (all Barcelona) ⚽ DFB Pokal: 2017 (Borussia Dortmund)

INTERNATIONAL HONORS

⚽ FIFA World Cup: 2018, runner-up 2022

⚽ UEFA Nations League third place: 2025

ACTIVITY AREAS

NATIONALITY
Portugal

CURRENT CLUB
Manchester United

BRUNO FERNANDES

Bruno Fernandes shines as a central or attacking midfielder, but is comfortable playing in a defensive mode too. He has a fantastic eye for creating chances with through balls, driving powerful shots from long range, and is a master at converting penalties and free kicks.

DATE OF BIRTH	SEP 08, 1994
POSITION	ATTACKING
HEIGHT	5 FT. 10 IN.
PRO DEBUT	2012
PREFERRED FOOT	RIGHT

APPEARANCES 396

ASSISTS 92

DRIBBLES 684

PENALTIES SCORED 38

PASSES 17,939

SUCCESSFUL PASSES 77.9%

GOALS 111

SHOTS 989

CHANCES CREATED 907

TACKLES 645

*Excludes data from Portuguese Premeira League

MAJOR CLUB HONORS

⚽ UEFA Europa League: runner-up 2021, runner-up 2025 ⚽ Taça de Portugal: 2019 (Sporting CP) ⚽ Taça de Liga: 2018, 2019 (Sporting CP) ⚽ FA Cup: runner-up 2023, 2024

INTERNATIONAL HONORS

⚽ UEFA Nations League: 2019, 2025

ACTIVITY AREAS

ENZO FERNÁNDEZ

The Argentinian has enjoyed a meteoric rise, most notably picking up the FIFA Best Young Player award at the 2022 World Cup. Playing in central midfield, he is happy to help his defenders, while his exceptionally accurate long-range passing often launches dangerous attacks.

NATIONALITY
Argentina

CURRENT CLUB
Chelsea

DATE OF BIRTH	JAN 17, 2001
POSITION	CENTRAL
HEIGHT	5 FT. 10 IN.
PRO DEBUT	2019
PREFERRED FOOT	RIGHT

APPEARANCES 97*

ASSISTS 18

DRIBBLES 141

PENALTIES SCORED 1

PASSES 5,846

SUCCESSFUL PASSES 86.8%

GOALS 11

SHOTS 144

CHANCES CREATED 146

TACKLES 193

*Excludes data from Argentinian and Portuguese Leagues

MAJOR CLUB HONORS
⚽ UEFA Conference League: 2025 ⚽ EFL Cup: 2025 ⚽ FIFA World Club Cup: 2025 ⚽ Argentina Primera División: 2021 (River Plate)

INTERNATIONAL HONORS
⚽ FIFA World Cup: 2022
⚽ Copa América: 2024

ACTIVITY AREAS

YOUSSOUF FOFANA

A commanding presence in the middle of the park, Youssouf Fofana plays a key role for both club and country. He is known for his box-to-box presence and is comfortable taking a leadership role, orchestrating the play and controlling the tempo of the match.

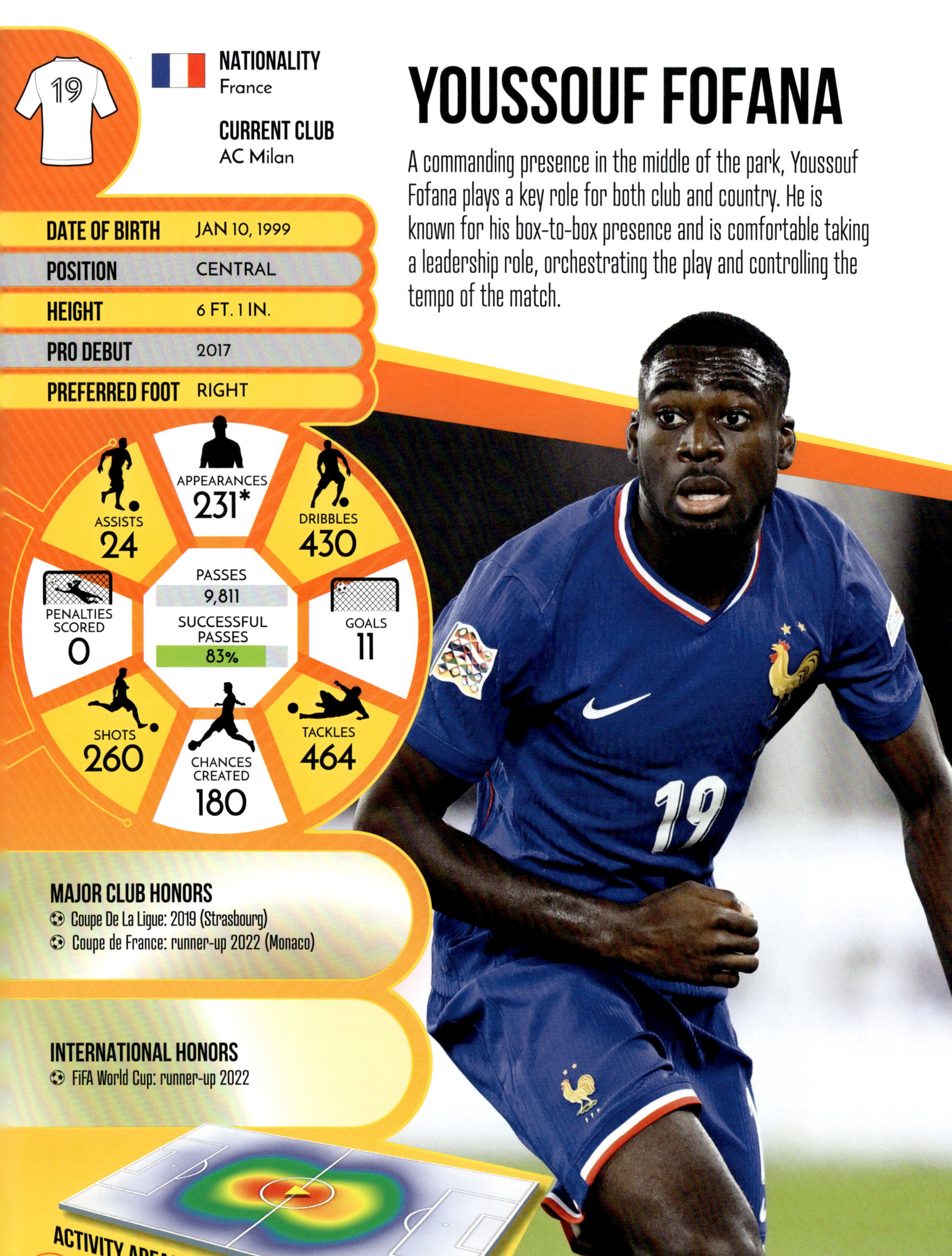

19

NATIONALITY
France

CURRENT CLUB
AC Milan

DATE OF BIRTH	JAN 10, 1999
POSITION	CENTRAL
HEIGHT	6 FT. 1 IN.
PRO DEBUT	2017
PREFERRED FOOT	RIGHT

APPEARANCES 231*

DRIBBLES 430

GOALS 11

TACKLES 464

CHANCES CREATED 180

SHOTS 260

PENALTIES SCORED 0

ASSISTS 24

PASSES 9,811

SUCCESSFUL PASSES 83%

MAJOR CLUB HONORS

- Coupe De La Ligue: 2019 (Strasbourg)
- Coupe de France: runner-up 2022 (Monaco)

INTERNATIONAL HONORS

- FIFA World Cup: runner-up 2022

ACTIVITY AREAS

İLKAY GÜNDOĞAN

Although İlkay Gündoğan became a superstar quite late on in his career, his teammates have always recognized his value. Admired for his solid defensive talent, great energy, passing ability, and reading of the game, he often dictates the flow and tempo of a match.

NATIONALITY
Germany

CURRENT CLUB
Manchester City

DATE OF BIRTH	OCT 24, 1990
POSITION	CENTRAL
HEIGHT	5 FT. 11 IN.
PRO DEBUT	2008
PREFERRED FOOT	RIGHT

APPEARANCES 522

ASSISTS 62

DRIBBLES 921

PENALTIES SCORED 5

PASSES 29,002

SUCCESSFUL PASSES 89.4%

GOALS 79

SHOTS 734

CHANCES CREATED 664

TACKLES 644

MAJOR CLUB HONORS

⚽ UEFA Champions League: 2023, runner-up 2021, runner-up 2013 (B. Dortmund) ⚽ Premier League: 2018, 2019, 2021-23 ⚽ Bundesliga: 2012 (B. Dortmund) ⚽ FA Cup: 2018, 2019, runner-up 2025 ⚽ DFB-Pokal: 2012 (B. Dortmund)

INTERNATIONAL HONORS

⚽ None to date

ACTIVITY AREAS

FRENKIE DE JONG

Frenkie de Jong has been an outstanding talent ever since he burst onto the scene as a teenager. His close control, work rate, passing accuracy, and movement have seen him being compared to the great Johan Cruyff.

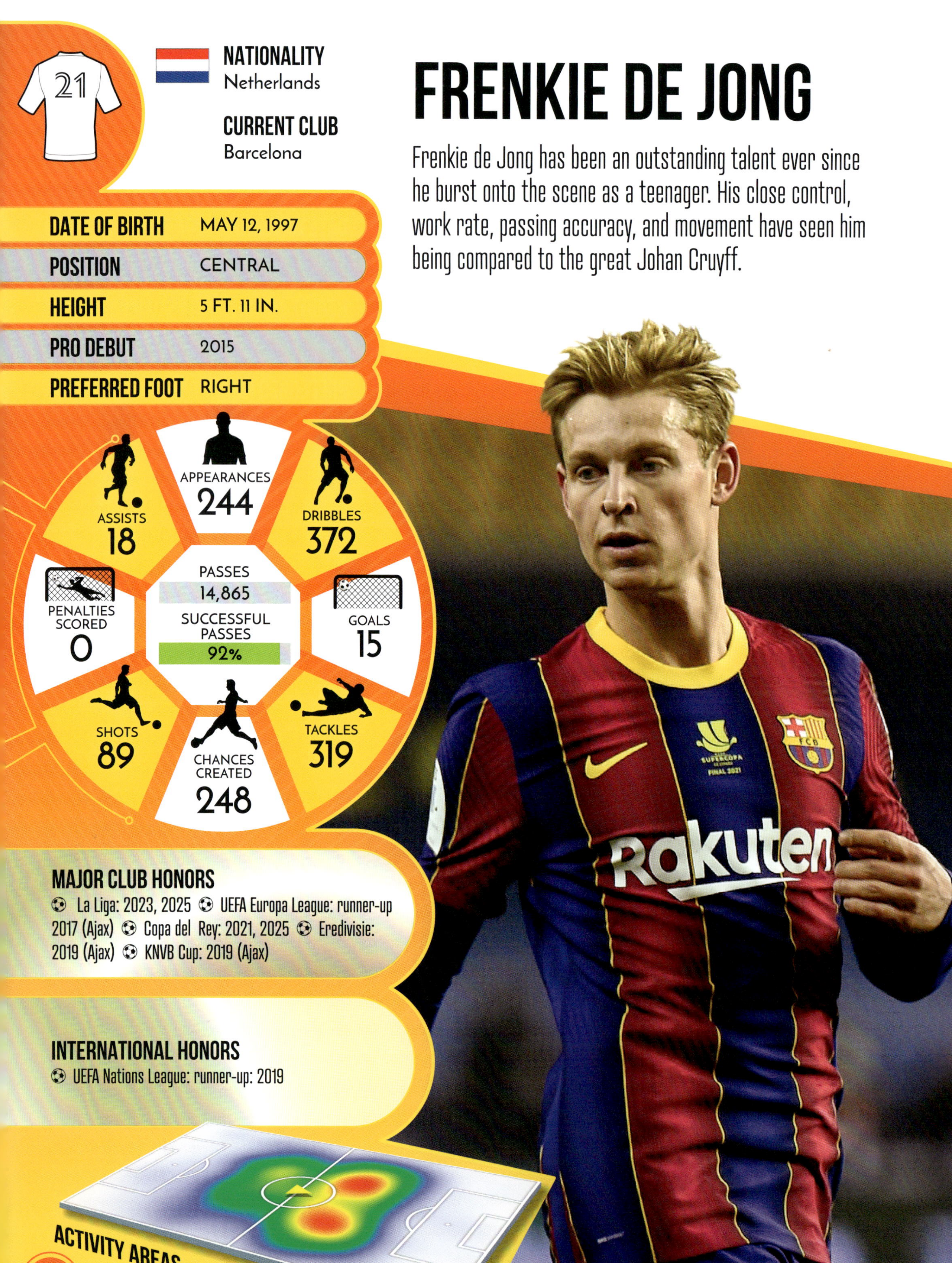

MAJOR CLUB HONORS

⚽ La Liga: 2023, 2025 ⚽ UEFA Europa League: runner-up 2017 (Ajax) ⚽ Copa del Rey: 2021, 2025 ⚽ Eredivisie: 2019 (Ajax) ⚽ KNVB Cup: 2019 (Ajax)

INTERNATIONAL HONORS

⚽ UEFA Nations League: runner-up: 2019

JORGINHO

The talented Jorginho can control the tempo of play from deep, linking defense with midfield, and can even advance up the field and reach attackers with his accurate passing. He has the awareness, vision, and passing ability to break lines, and can deliver lofted balls into the danger areas.

NATIONALITY
Italy

CURRENT CLUB
Arsenal

DATE OF BIRTH	DEC 20, 1991
POSITION	DEFENSIVE
HEIGHT	5 FT. 11 IN.
PRO DEBUT	2010
PREFERRED FOOT	BOTH

APPEARANCES 425
ASSISTS 28
DRIBBLES 297
PASSES 29,162
SUCCESSFUL PASSES 89.3%
PENALTIES SCORED 35
GOALS 40
SHOTS 179
CHANCES CREATED 400
TACKLES 820

MAJOR CLUB HONORS

- Premier League: runner-up 2023, runner-up 2024, runner-up 2025
- UEFA Champs League: 2021 (Chelsea)
- UEFA Europa League: 2019 (Chelsea)
- FIFA World Club Cup: 2021 (Chelsea)
- FA Cup: runner-up 2020-22 (Chelsea)
- Coppa Italia: 2014 (Napoli)

INTERNATIONAL HONORS

- UEFA European Championship: 2020
- UEFA Nations League: third place 2021, third place 2023

ACTIVITY AREAS

NATIONALITY
Argentina

CURRENT CLUB
Liverpool

ALEXIS MAC ALLISTER

Alexis Mac Allister is a versatile midfielder, equally efficient in central, attacking, or defensive roles. He has great positional awareness, allowing him to break up attacks and then playing long, accurate downfield passes to teammates in dangerous forward positions.

DATE OF BIRTH	DEC 24, 1998
POSITION	CENTRAL
HEIGHT	5 FT. 9 IN.
PRO DEBUT	2016
PREFERRED FOOT	RIGHT

APPEARANCES 180

ASSISTS 17

DRIBBLES 232

PENALTIES SCORED 10

PASSES 7,280

SUCCESSFUL PASSES 86.5%

GOALS 29

SHOTS 272

CHANCES CREATED 213

TACKLES 391

MAJOR CLUB HONORS

- Premier League: 2025
- EFL Cup: 2024, runner-up 2025

INTERNATIONAL HONORS

- FIFA World Cup: 2022
- Copa América: 2024
- CONMEBOL—UEFA Cup of Champions: 2022

ACTIVITY AREAS

WESTON MCKENNIE

Tough and competitive on the field, Weston McKennie is a ball-winning midfielder with an instinct to break up play and interrupt the flow of the opposition. He likes making late runs into the box to join attacks, plus offers another weapon in attack—his extraordinarily long throws.

NATIONALITY
USA

CURRENT CLUB
Juventus

DATE OF BIRTH	AUG 28, 1998
POSITION	CENTRAL
HEIGHT	6 FT. 1 IN.
PRO DEBUT	2017
PREFERRED FOOT	RIGHT

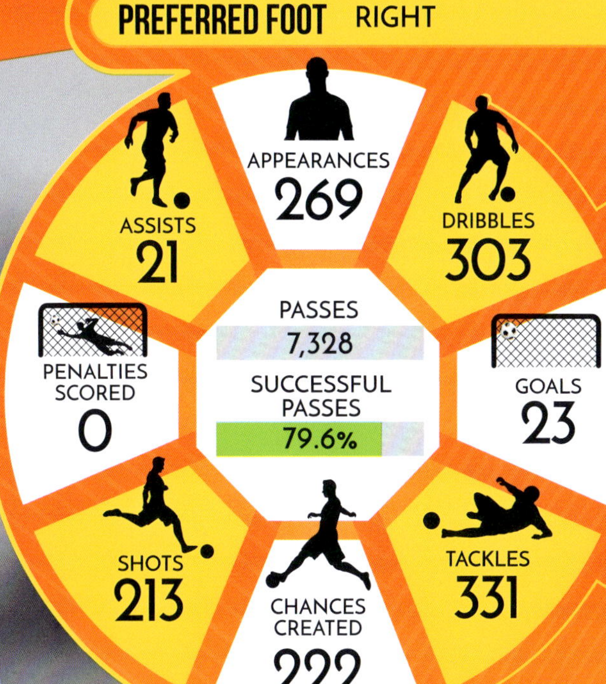

MAJOR CLUB HONORS
- Coppa Italia: 202, 2024

INTERNATIONAL HONORS
- CONCACAF Nations League: 2020, 2023, 2024
- CONCACAF Gold Cup: runner-up: 2019

ACTIVITY AREAS

NATIONALITY
Croatia

CURRENT CLUB
AC Milan

LUKA MODRIĆ

A top player for more than 20 years (13 seasons with Real Madrid) and a Ballon d'Or winner in 2018, Luka Modrić is still capable of moments of magic on the field. He has a great soccer sense, can deliver long and short passes with both feet, and can strike powerful long-range shots, especially free kicks.

DATE OF BIRTH	SEP 09, 1985
POSITION	ATTACKING
HEIGHT	5 FT. 8 IN.
PRO DEBUT	2003
PREFERRED FOOT	RIGHT

APPEARANCES 677

DRIBBLES 1513

GOALS 53

TACKLES 842

CHANCES CREATED 1,057

SHOTS 765

PENALTIES SCORED 5

ASSISTS 99

PASSES 37,487

SUCCESSFUL PASSES 89.2%

MAJOR CLUB HONORS

- La Liga: 2017, 2020, 2022 (all Real Madrid)
- UEFA Champions League: 2014, 2016, 2017, 2018, 2022, 2024 (all R. Mad.)
- UEFA Super Cup: 2014, 2016, 2017, 2022 (all R. Mad.)
- FIFA Club World Cup: 2014, 2016, 2017, 2018, 2022 (all R. Mad.)
- Copa del Rey: 2014, 2023 (all R. Mad.)

INTERNATIONAL HONORS

- FIFA World Cup: runner-up 2018, third place 2022
- UEFA Nations League: runner-up 2023

ACTIVITY AREAS

THOMAS MÜLLER

Thomas Müller is a dangerous attacking midfielder, who scores countless goals playing just behind a lone striker. The German powerhouse is mentally strong, tactically clever, and great at finding holes in the opposition's defence. In 2025, he left Bayern Munich after 25 years with the club.

NATIONALITY
Germany

CURRENT CLUB
TBC

DATE OF BIRTH	SEP 13, 1989
POSITION	SECOND STRIKER
HEIGHT	6 FT. 1 IN.
PRO DEBUT	2008
PREFERRED FOOT	RIGHT

APPEARANCES 668

ASSISTS 198

DRIBBLES 1,072

PENALTIES SCORED 22

PASSES 20,852

SUCCESSFUL PASSES 76.9%

GOALS 207

SHOTS 1,245

CHANCES CREATED 1,222

TACKLES 664

MAJOR CLUB HONORS

⚽ Bundesliga: 2010, 2013, 2014, 2015, 2016, 2017, 2018, 2019, 2020, 2021, 2022, 2023, 2025 ⚽ DFB-Pokal: 2010, 2013, 2014, 2016, 2019, 2020 ⚽ UEFA Champions League: runner-up 2010, runner-up 2012, 2013, 2020 ⚽ FIFA Club World Cup: 2013, 2020

INTERNATIONAL HONORS

⚽ FIFA World Cup: 2014, third place 2010
⚽ UEFA European Championship: third place 2012

ACTIVITY AREAS

NATIONALITY
Germany

CURRENT CLUB
Bayern Munich

JAMAL MUSIALA

Among the new generation of mega stars at Bayern, Jamal Musiala is a big-game player, famed for his exceptional pace and quick feet. Easy on the eye, he can dribble past defenders, find teammates with inch-perfect passes, and unleash powerful shots from any distance.

DATE OF BIRTH	FEB 26, 2003
POSITION	ATTACKING/WINGER
HEIGHT	6 FT.
PRO DEBUT	2020
PREFERRED FOOT	RIGHT

MAJOR CLUB HONORS
⚽ Bundesliga: 2020, 2021, 2022, 2023, 2025 ⚽ UEFA Champions League: 2020 ⚽ FIFA Club World Cup: 2020

INTERNATIONAL HONORS
⚽ None to date

ACTIVITY AREAS

COLE PALMER

Although Cole Palmer is naturally left-footed, he is more than capable with his right, which makes him a strong dribbler who can unlock the tightest defenses. Mentally strong andbrimming with confidence, he strikes the ball sweetly, especially on penalties and free kicks.

NATIONALITY
England

CURRENT CLUB
Chelsea

DATE OF BIRTH	MAY 06, 2002
POSITION	ATTACKING
HEIGHT	6 FT. 1 IN.
PRO DEBUT	2020
PREFERRED FOOT	LEFT

APPEARANCES 104

DRIBBLES 258

GOALS 39

TACKLES 74

CHANCES CREATED 177

SHOTS 273

PENALTIES SCORED 13

ASSISTS 23

PASSES 3,192

SUCCESSFUL PASSES 84%

MAJOR CLUB HONORS

⚽ Premier League: 2023 (Man. City) ⚽ UEFA Champions League: 2023 (Man. City) ⚽ FIFA World Club Cup: 2025 ⚽ UEFA Conference League: 2025 ⚽ FA Cup: 2023 (Man. City)

INTERNATIONAL HONORS

⚽ UEFA European Championship: runner-up 2024

ACTIVITY AREAS

NATIONALITY
USA

CURRENT CLUB
AC Milan

CHRISTIAN PULISIC

Although capable of playing in any attacking position, Christian Pulisic has recently been operating as a winger where he shows off his speed, strength, and decision-making. He can run past defenders, inside or out, make dangerous runs into the penalty area, and score goals.

DATE OF BIRTH	SEP 18, 1998
POSITION	RIGHT
HEIGHT	5 FT. 10 IN.
PRO DEBUT	2016
PREFERRED FOOT	BOTH

ASSISTS
52

APPEARANCES
335

DRIBBLES
1253

PENALTIES SCORED
3

PASSES
7,686

SUCCESSFUL PASSES
81%

GOALS
70

SHOTS
485

CHANCES CREATED
365

TACKLES
311

MAJOR CLUB HONORS

⚽ UEFA Champions League: 2021 (Chelsea) ⚽ UEFA Super Cup: 2021 (Chelsea) ⚽ FIFA Club World Cup: 2021 (Chelsea) ⚽ DFB-Pokal: 2017 (Borussia Dortmund)

INTERNATIONAL HONORS

⚽ CONCACAF Nations League: 2020, 2023, 2024
⚽ ONCACAF Gold Cup: runner-up 2019

ACTIVITY AREAS

DECLAN RICE

Declan Rice has long been considered an exceptional defensive midfielder; now he has found an attacking flair playing in central midfield. He has added fine ball skills, passing, crossing, and long-range shooting to his athleticism and tackling ability.

NATIONALITY
England

CURRENT CLUB
Arsenal

DATE OF BIRTH	JAN 14, 1999
POSITION	RIGHT
HEIGHT	6 FT. 2 IN.
PRO DEBUT	2017
PREFERRED FOOT	RIGHT

APPEARANCES 321

ASSISTS 29

DRIBBLES 415

PENALTIES SCORED 1

PASSES 15,358

SUCCESSFUL PASSES 88.7%

GOALS 29

SHOTS 296

CHANCES CREATED 254

TACKLES 681

MAJOR CLUB HONORS
- Premier League: runner-up 2024, runner-up 2025
- UEFA Europa Conference League: 2023 (West Ham Utd)

INTERNATIONAL HONORS
- UEFA European Championship: runner-up 2020 (2021), runner-up 2024
- UEFA Nations League: (third place) 2019

ACTIVITY AREAS

NATIONALITY
England

CURRENT CLUB
Arsenal

BUKAYO SAKA

A rising star in world soccer, Buyako Saka's versatility is just one of his talents. Equally good on both sides at full-back or wing-back, his creativity, positional sense, tackling, shooting, and passing talents are displayed best as a right midfielder.

DATE OF BIRTH	SEP 05, 2001
POSITION	WINGER
HEIGHT	5 FT. 10 IN.
PRO DEBUT	2018
PREFERRED FOOT	LEFT

ASSISTS
59

APPEARANCES
238

DRIBBLES
752

PENALTIES SCORED
12

PASSES
6,981

SUCCESSFUL PASSES
82%

GOALS
68

SHOTS
510

CHANCES CREATED
413

TACKLES
312

MAJOR CLUB HONORS

⚽ Premier League: runner-up 2023, runner-up 2024, runner-up 2025 ⚽ FA Cup: 2020 ⚽ UEFA Europa League: runner-up 2019

INTERNATIONAL HONORS

⚽ UEFA European Championship: runner-up 2020 (2021), runner-up 2024

ACTIVITY AREAS

LEROY SANÉ

Leroy Sané is almost the perfect example of a right-winger, except his left foot is stronger. He has all the other attributes to be fearsome on the flanks: great ball control, fine positional and tactical sense, top-class dribbling, and outstanding pace to beat defenders.

NATIONALITY
Germany

CURRENT CLUB
Galatasaray (Turkey)

DATE OF BIRTH	JAN 11, 1996
POSITION	WINGER
HEIGHT	6 FT.
PRO DEBUT	2014
PREFERRED FOOT	LEFT

APPEARANCES
371

ASSISTS
90

DRIBBLES
1,651

PENALTIES SCORED
0

PASSES
10,317

SUCCESSFUL PASSES
83.3%

GOALS
100

SHOTS
783

CHANCES CREATED
510

TACKLES
382

MAJOR CLUB HONORS

⚽ Bundesliga: 2021, 2022, 2023, 2025 (all B. Munich) ⚽ FIFA Club World Cup: 2020 2021 (all B. Munich) ⚽ UEFA Super Cup: 2020 (B. Munich) ⚽ Premier League: 2018, 2019 (all Man. City) ⚽ FA Cup: 2019 (Man. City)

INTERNATIONAL HONORS

⚽ FIFA Confederations Cup: 2017

ACTIVITY AREAS

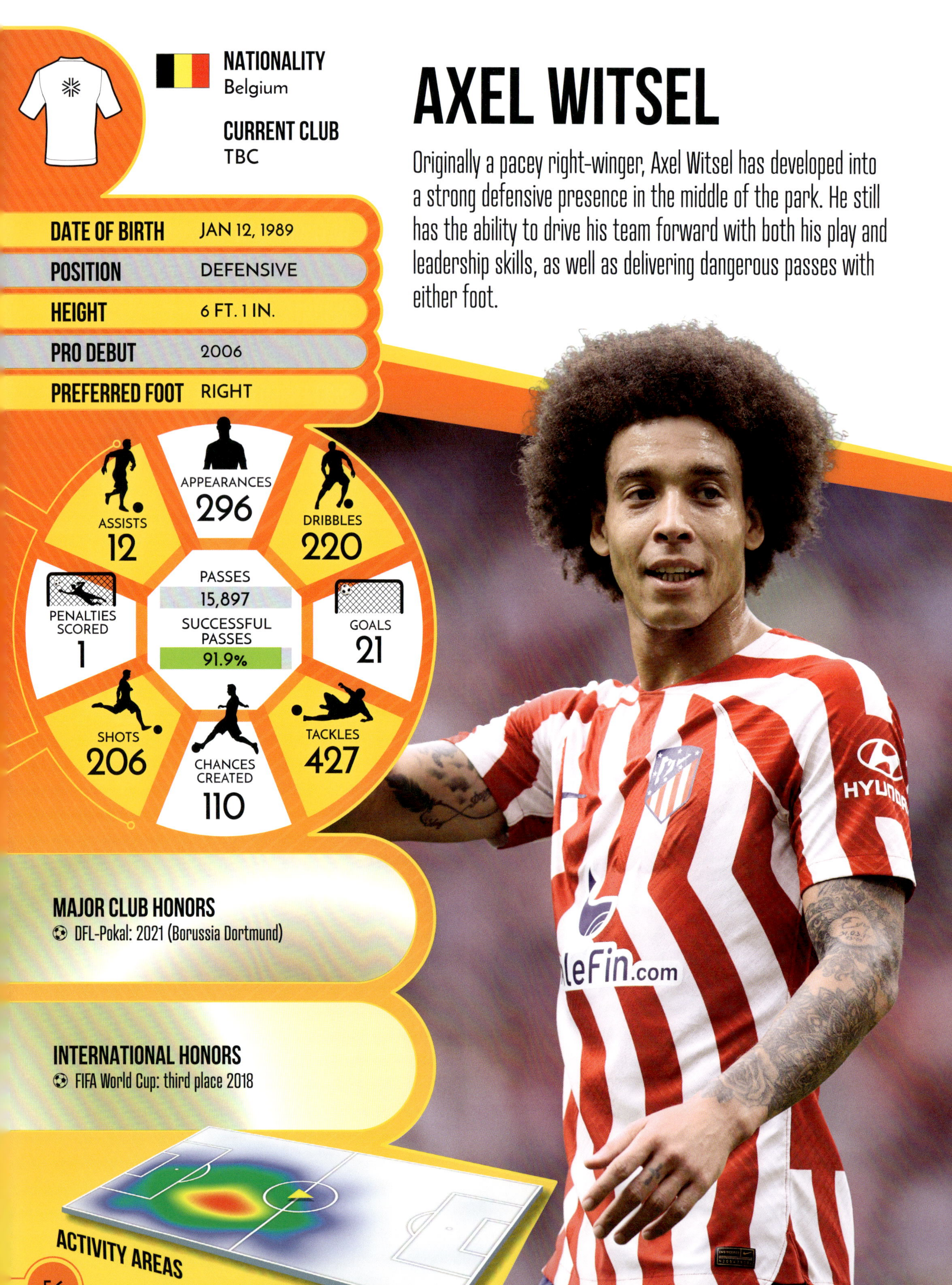

AXEL WITSEL

NATIONALITY
Belgium

CURRENT CLUB
TBC

Originally a pacey right-winger, Axel Witsel has developed into a strong defensive presence in the middle of the park. He still has the ability to drive his team forward with both his play and leadership skills, as well as delivering dangerous passes with either foot.

DATE OF BIRTH	JAN 12, 1989
POSITION	DEFENSIVE
HEIGHT	6 FT. 1 IN.
PRO DEBUT	2006
PREFERRED FOOT	RIGHT

APPEARANCES 296
DRIBBLES 220
GOALS 21
TACKLES 427
CHANCES CREATED 110
SHOTS 206
PENALTIES SCORED 1
ASSISTS 12
PASSES 15,897
SUCCESSFUL PASSES 91.9%

MAJOR CLUB HONORS

- DFL-Pokal: 2021 (Borussia Dortmund)

INTERNATIONAL HONORS

- FIFA World Cup: third place 2018

ACTIVITY AREAS

GRANIT XHAKA

Granit Xhaka makes any team he plays for much harder to break down with his performances in defensive midfield. One of the fittest players around, he combines boundless energy with great positional sense and fine tackling technique, and opponents must respect his long-range shooting ability.

NATIONALITY
Switzerland

CURRENT CLUB
Bayer Leverkusen

DATE OF BIRTH	SEP 27, 1992
POSITION	DEFENSIVE
HEIGHT	6 FT. 1 IN.
PRO DEBUT	2010
PREFERRED FOOT	LEFT

APPEARANCES 494

DRIBBLES 489

GOALS 34

TACKLES 865

CHANCES CREATED 502

SHOTS 532

PENALTIES SCORED 1

ASSISTS 41

PASSES 34,461

SUCCESSFUL PASSES 88.1%

MAJOR CLUB HONORS

⚽ Bundesliga: 2024 ⚽ UEFA Europa League: runner-up 2019 (Arsenal), runner-up 2024 ⚽ DFB-Pokal: 2024 ⚽ FA Cup: 2017, 2020 (Arsenal) ⚽ Swiss Super League: 2011, 2012 (all Basel)

INTERNATIONAL HONORS

⚽ None to date

ACTIVITY AREAS

FORWARDS

The forwards are a team's frontline attackers and the chief goal scorers. They are also the team's most celebrated players. Whether it is the smaller, quicker player, such as Neymar and Mohamed Salah, or the bigger, more physical attacker, such as Erling Haaland and Romelu Lukaku, strikers have perfected the art of finding the back of the net on a regular basis. Aside from scoring lots of goals, the world's best strikers are also effective at creating chances for their teammates.

WHAT DO THE STATS MEAN?

GOALS

This is the total number of goals a striker has scored. The figure spans across all the top clubs the player has represented so far in their career.

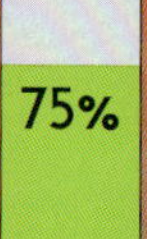

CONVERSION RATE

The percentage shows how good the player is at taking their chance in front of goal. If a player scores two goals from four shots, their conversion rate is 50 percent.

ASSISTS

A pass, cross, or header to a teammate who then scores counts as an assist. This stat also includes a deflected shot that is immediately converted by a teammate.

128

MINUTES PER GOAL

This is the average length of time it takes for the player to score. It is calculated across all the minutes the player has played in their career at top level.

Did you know?

A perfect hat-trick is one where the player scores one goal with his right foot, another with his left foot, and a third with his head. It does not matter in which order the goals come.

JONATHAN DAVID

Jonathan David is a live wire on the field who combines speed, balance, and excellent ball control. Normally used as second striker, feeding off a target man, he has a talent for finding holes in opposing defenses, through which he can run or deliver inch-perfect passes.

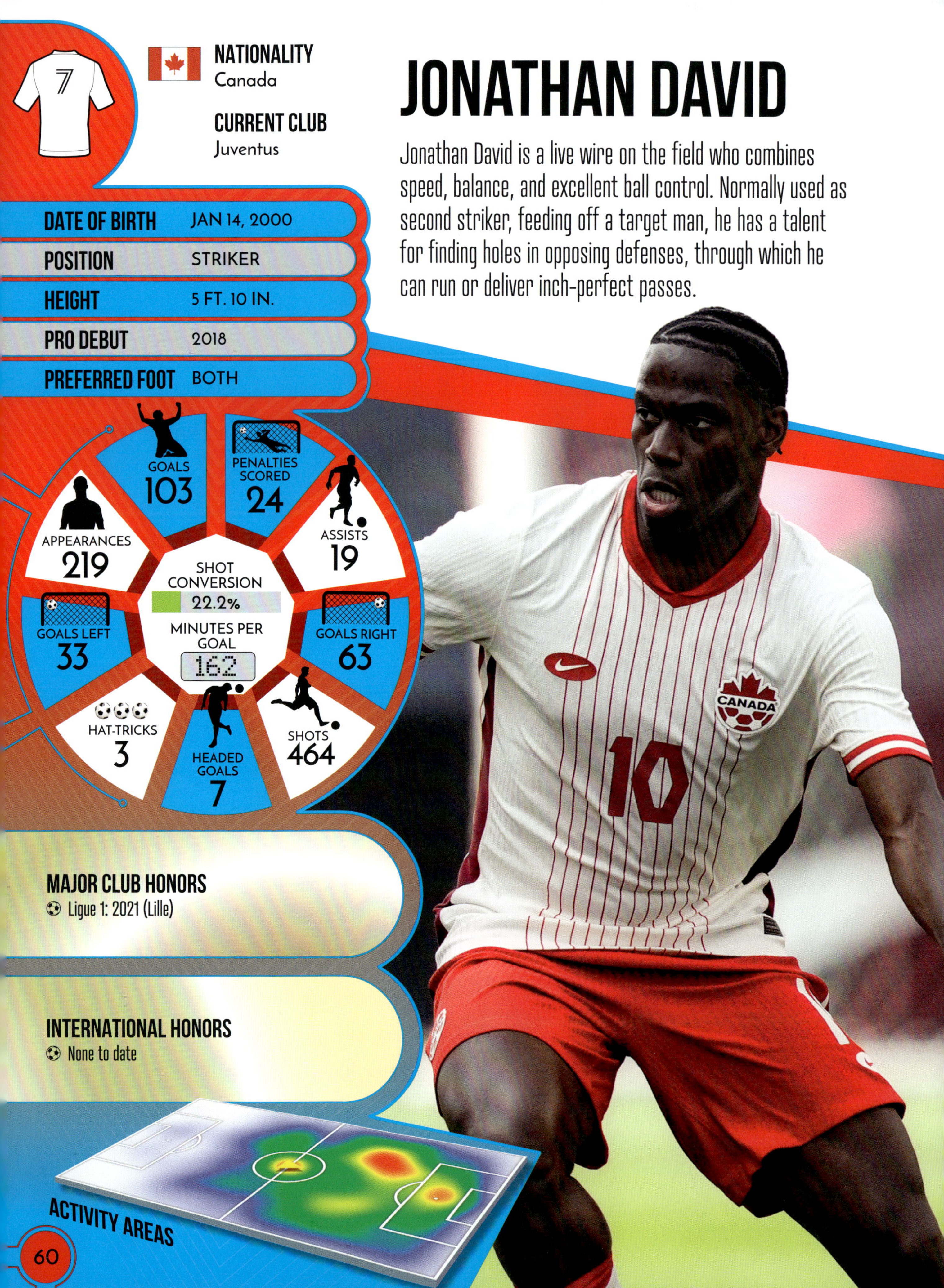

MEMPHIS DEPAY

Memphis Depay is a striker who plays with intensity. He is an exceptional dribbler too and can play as a left-winger or left-sided striker. He is a brave player and will challenge the biggest defenders in the middle of the danger area.

NATIONALITY
Netherlands

CURRENT CLUB
Corinthians (Brazil)

DATE OF BIRTH	FEB 13, 1994
POSITION	WINGER
HEIGHT	5 FT. 10 IN.
PRO DEBUT	2011
PREFERRED FOOT	RIGHT

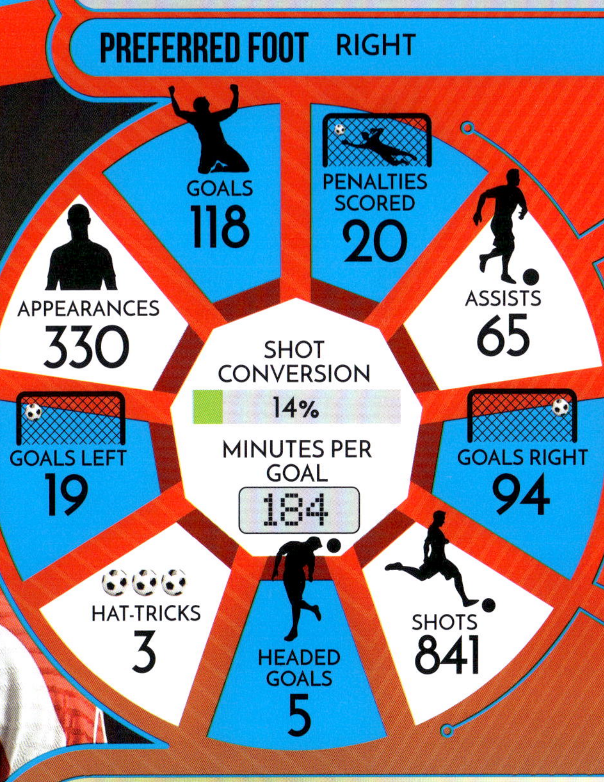

MAJOR CLUB HONORS
⚽ La Liga: 2023 (Barcelona) ⚽ Eredivisie: 2015 (PSV Eindhoven) ⚽ KNVB Cup: 2012 (PSV Eindhoven) ⚽ Coupe de La Ligue: runner-up 2020 (Lyon)

INTERNATIONAL HONORS
⚽ FIFA World Cup: third place 2014

ACTIVITY AREAS

JOÃO FÉLIX

Portugal's João Félix has developed into a technically gifted and intelligent goal scorer. Probably at his best as a second striker, linking with the midfield and making late runs into the box, he has good vision, control, dribbling skills, and passing ability.

MAJOR CLUB HONORS

- FIFA World Club Cup: 2025
- La Liga: 2021 (Atlético Madrid)
- Primeira Liga: 2019 (Benfica)

INTERNATIONAL HONORS

- UEFA Nations League: 2019, 2025

PHIL FODEN

Phil Foden can play in many positions: on either wing or centrally as a striker or playmaking midfielder. Naturally left-footed, he has an exceptional first touch, close control, poise, balance, tactical awareness, a powerful shot, pace, and stamina. He can be a game winner on his day!

NATIONALITY
England

CURRENT CLUB
Manchester City

DATE OF BIRTH	MAY 28, 2000
POSITION	SECOND STRIKER
HEIGHT	5 FT. 7 IN.
PRO DEBUT	2016
PREFERRED FOOT	LEFT

GOALS 79

PENALTIES SCORED 0

ASSISTS 40

APPEARANCES 254

SHOT CONVERSION 16%

MINUTES PER GOAL 198

GOALS LEFT 61

GOALS RIGHT 15

HAT-TRICKS 3

HEADED GOALS 3

SHOTS 495

MAJOR CLUB HONORS
- Premier League: 2018, 2019, 2021, 2022, 2023, 2024
- UEFA Champions League: 2023, runners-up 2021
- UEFA Super Cup: 2023
- FIFA Club World Cup: 2023
- FA Cup: 2019, 2023, runner-up 2024

INTERNATIONAL HONORS
- UEFA European Championship: runner-up 2020, 2024

ACTIVITY AREAS

NATIONALITY
France

CURRENT CLUB
Los Angeles FC (USA)

OLIVIER GIROUD

Olivier Giroud is much more than a target man because his work-rate and positional sense make him hard to defend against near the goal. He uses his physique to hold and shield the ball, and is known for his accurate passing, shooting, and heading.

DATE OF BIRTH	SEP 30, 1986
POSITION	STRIKER
HEIGHT	6 FT. 4 IN.
PRO DEBUT	2005
PREFERRED FOOT	LEFT

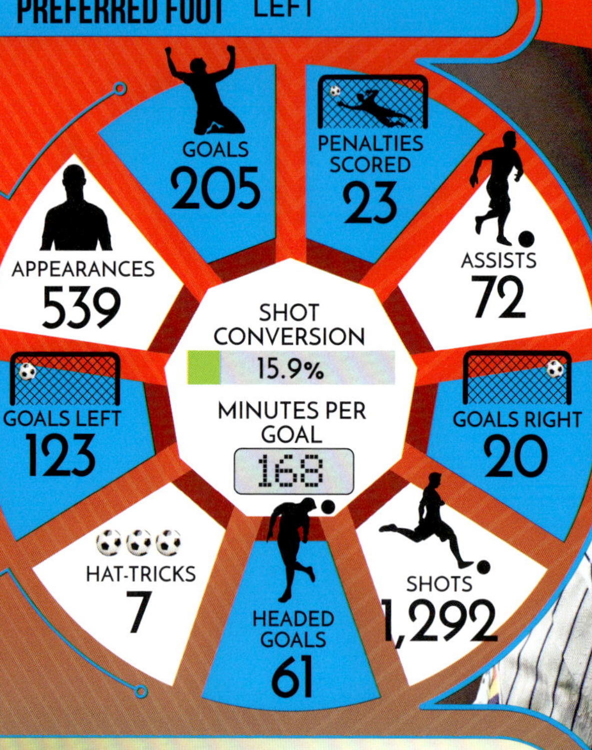

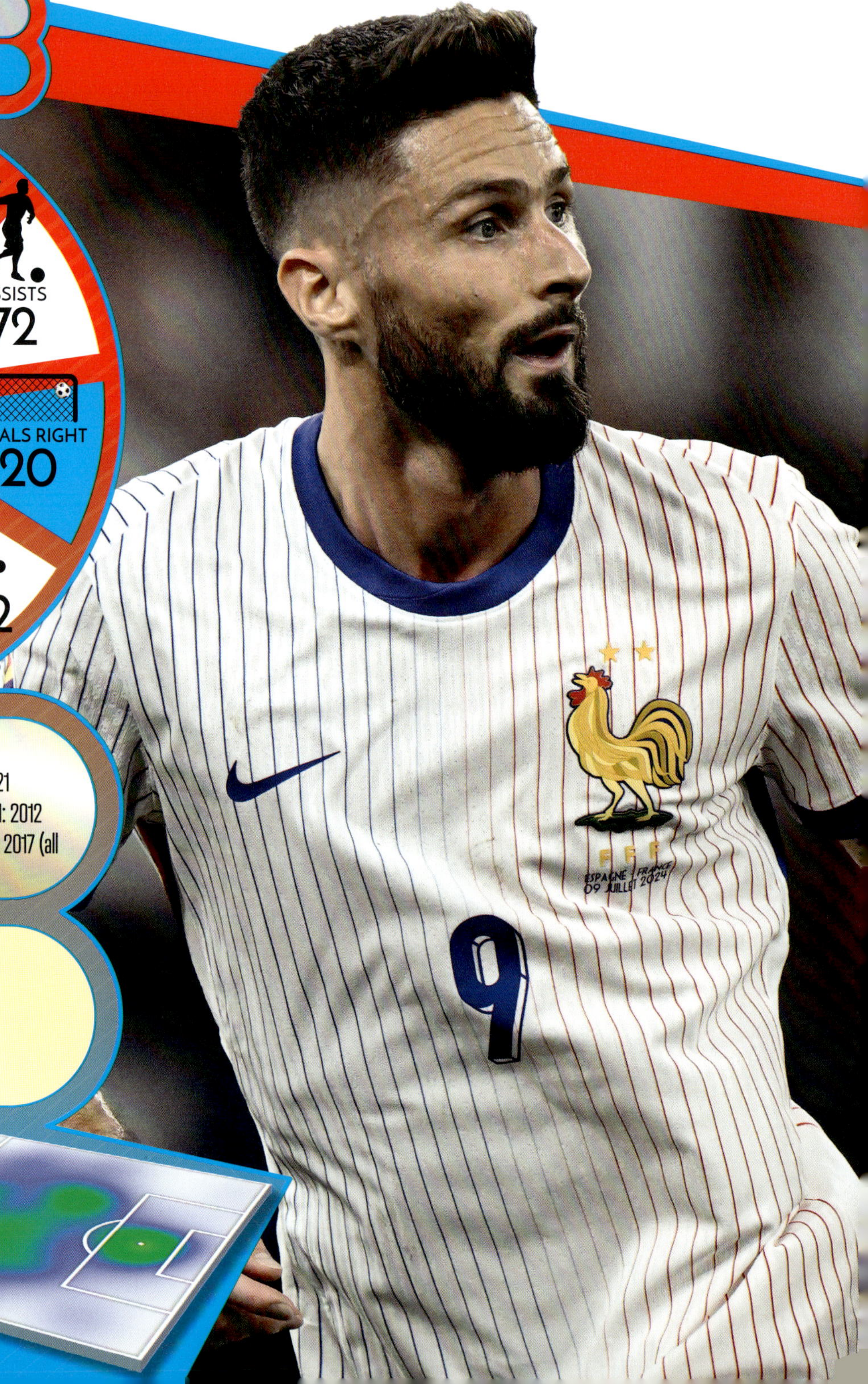

MAJOR CLUB HONORS

⚽ Serie A: 2022 (AC Milan) ⚽ UEFA Champions League: 2021 (Chelsea) ⚽ UEFA Europa League: 2019 (Chelsea) ⚽ Ligue 1: 2012 (Montpellier) ⚽ US Open Cup: 2024 ⚽ FA Cup: 2014, 2015, 2017 (all Arsenal), 2018 (Chelsea) 2017 (Arsenal), 2018 (Chelsea)

INTERNATIONAL HONORS

⚽ FIFA World Cup 2018, runner-up 2022
⚽ UEFA European Championship: runner-up 2016

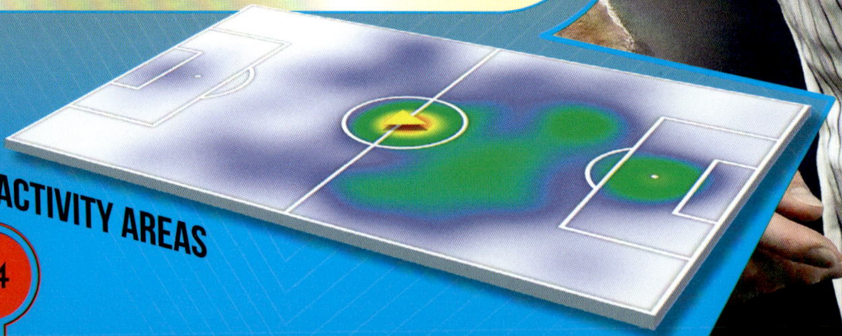

ACTIVITY AREAS

ANTOINE GRIEZMANN

Known for being the ultimate team player, Antoine Griezmann is able to take on all offensive roles, be it as a front man, attacking midfielder, false NO.9, or coming from wide positions. He is an excellent teammate, using his experience to get the best out of everyone on the field.

NATIONALITY
France

CURRENT CLUB
Atlético Madrid

DATE OF BIRTH	MAR 21, 1991
POSITION	STRIKER
HEIGHT	5 FT. 9 IN.
PRO DEBUT	2009
PREFERRED FOOT	LEFT

MAJOR CLUB HONORS
- UEFA Champions League: runner-up 2016
- UEFA Europa League 2018
- UEFA Super Cup 2018
- Copa del Rey 2021 (Barcelona)

INTERNATIONAL HONORS
- FIFA World Cup: 2018, runner-up 2022
- UEFA European Championship: runner-up 2016
- UEFA Nations League: 2021

ACTIVITY AREAS

NATIONALITY
Norway

CURRENT CLUB
Manchester City

ERLING HAALAND

Erling Haaland terrorizes defenses with his blistering pace, aerial ability, strength, energy, timing, and attacking instincts. He is tall, extremely fast, well-balanced, good with both feet, an excellent passer, and a powerful shooter in open play or at set pieces.

DATE OF BIRTH	JUL 21, 2000
POSITION	STRIKER
HEIGHT	6 FT. 4 IN.
PRO DEBUT	2015
PREFERRED FOOT	LEFT

MAJOR CLUB HONORS

⚽ Premier League: 2023, 2024 ⚽ UEFA Champions League: 2023 ⚽ DFB-Pokal: 2021 (Borussia Dortmund) ⚽ Austrian Bundesliga: 2019, 2020 (Red Bull Salzburg) ⚽ FA Cup: 2023, runner-up 2024, runner-up 2025 ⚽ Austrian Cup: 2019 (Red Bull Salzburg)

INTERNATIONAL HONORS

⚽ None to date

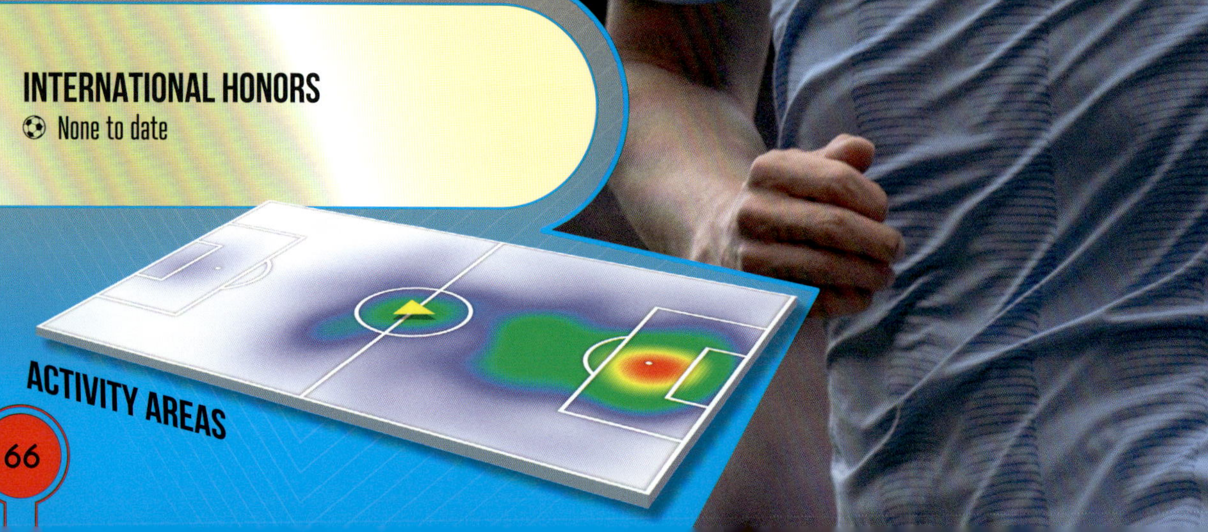

ALEXANDER ISAK

Alexander Isak is a complete striker, scoring and setting up goals with both feet and his head. He displays speed of thought and movement, together with great positional sense and timing, as well as helping out in defense when necessary.

NATIONALITY
Sweden

CURRENT CLUB
Newcastle

DATE OF BIRTH	SEP 21, 1999
POSITION	STRIKER
HEIGHT	6 FT. 3 IN.
PRO DEBUT	2016
PREFERRED FOOT	RIGHT

GOALS	91
PENALTIES SCORED	13
ASSISTS	14
GOALS RIGHT	66
SHOTS	472
HEADED GOALS	10
HAT-TRICKS	2
GOALS LEFT	15
APPEARANCES	219
SHOT CONVERSION	19.3%
MINUTES PER GOAL	155

MAJOR CLUB HONORS

⚽ Football League Cup: 2025 ⚽ Copa del Rey 2020 (Real Sociedad) ⚽ DFB-Pokal: 2017 (Borussia Dortmund)

INTERNATIONAL HONORS

⚽ None to date

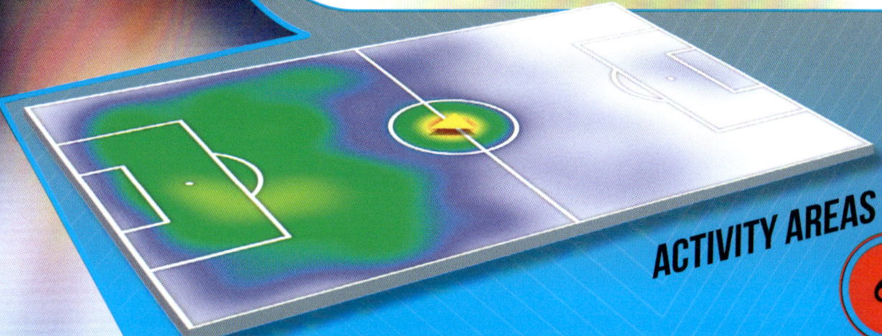

ACTIVITY AREAS

LUKA JOVIĆ

Luka Jović is a predator in the penalty box. He uses his speed and attacking instincts to find spaces in the penalty area and score goals from close range with deft touches from either foot and occasionally his head. He left AC Milan at the end of the 2024/25 season.

NATIONALITY
Serbia

CURRENT CLUB
TBC

DATE OF BIRTH	DEC 23, 1997
POSITION	STRIKER
HEIGHT	5 FT. 11 IN.
PRO DEBUT	2014
PREFERRED FOOT	RIGHT

GOALS 63
PENALTIES SCORED 1
ASSISTS 15
APPEARANCES 219
SHOT CONVERSION 16.4%
MINUTES PER GOAL 159
GOALS LEFT 20
GOALS RIGHT 28
HAT-TRICKS 1
HEADED GOALS 15
SHOTS 384

MAJOR CLUB HONORS

⚽ La Liga: 2020, 2022 (Real Madrid) ⚽ UEFA Champions League: 2022 (Real Madrid) ⚽ UEFA Conference League: runner-up 2023 (Fiorentina) ⚽ DFB-Pokal: 2018 (Eintracht Frankfurt)

INTERNATIONAL HONORS

⚽ None to date

ACTIVITY AREAS

HARRY KANE

Harry Kane has grown into the complete striker. His power in the air, skills with both feet, and superb ball-striking technique make him hard to defend against. What's more, with his defense-splitting passes, he also sets up many goals for his teammates.

NATIONALITY
England

CURRENT CLUB
Bayern Munich

DATE OF BIRTH	JUL 28, 1993
POSITION	STRIKER
HEIGHT	6 FT. 2 IN.
PRO DEBUT	2009
PREFERRED FOOT	RIGHT

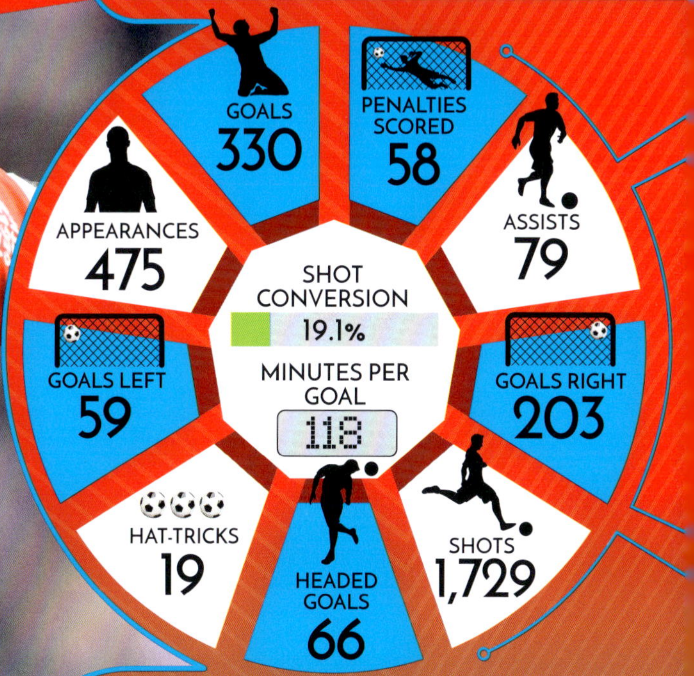

GOALS	330
PENALTIES SCORED	58
ASSISTS	79
GOALS RIGHT	203
SHOTS	1,729
HEADED GOALS	66
HAT-TRICKS	19
GOALS LEFT	59
APPEARANCES	475
SHOT CONVERSION	19.1%
MINUTES PER GOAL	118

MAJOR CLUB HONORS
⚽ Bundesliga: 2025 ⚽ UEFA Champions League: runner-up 2019 (Tottenham Hotspur)

INTERNATIONAL HONORS
⚽ UEFA European Championship: runner-up 2020 (2021), runner-up 2024 ⚽ UEFA Nations League: third place 2019

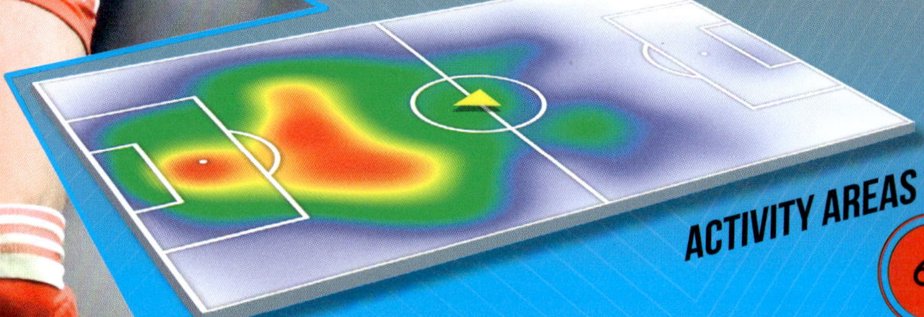

ACTIVITY AREAS

NATIONALITY
Poland

CURRENT CLUB
Barcelona

ROBERT LEWANDOWSKI

Robert Lewandowski has consistently ranked as one of the world's best strikers since he made his debut at Borussia Dortmund in 2010. His positioning, technique, power, and finishing saw him net more than 300 goals in the Bundesliga before he made his move to Barcelona in 2022.

DATE OF BIRTH	AUG 21, 1988
POSITION	STRIKER
HEIGHT	6 FT. 1 IN.
PRO DEBUT	2005
PREFERRED FOOT	RIGHT

GOALS 489
PENALTIES SCORED 67
ASSISTS 94
GOALS RIGHT 323
SHOTS 2,371
HEADED GOALS 78
HAT-TRICKS 24
GOALS LEFT 84
APPEARANCES 637
SHOT CONVERSION 20.6%
MINUTES PER GOAL 106

MAJOR CLUB HONORS

⚽ La Liga: 2023, 2025 ⚽ Bundesliga: 2011, 2012 (all B. Dortmund), 2015, '16, '17, '18, '19, '20, '21, '22 (all B. Munich) ⚽ UEFA Champions League: 2020 (B. Munich) ⚽ FIFA Club World Cup: 2020 (B. Munich) ⚽ Copa del Rey: 2025

INTERNATIONAL HONORS

⚽ None to date

ACTIVITY AREAS

ADEMOLA LOOKMAN

NATIONALITY
Nigeria

CURRENT CLUB
Atalanta

Ademola Lookman was raised in England, where he developed his skills, but it was in Italy that he achieved success in top-flight soccer. Creative, dynamic, direct, and with electric pace, he has quick feet, great control, a powerful shot with either foot, and is excellent in the air.

DATE OF BIRTH	OCT 20, 1997
POSITION	WINGER
HEIGHT	5 FT. 9 IN.
PRO DEBUT	2015
PREFERRED FOOT	BOTH

GOALS 67

PENALTIES SCORED 4

ASSISTS 34

GOALS RIGHT 45

SHOTS 165

HEADED GOALS 5

HAT-TRICKS 1

GOALS LEFT 17

APPEARANCES 249

SHOT CONVERSION 40.6%

MINUTES PER GOAL 214

MAJOR CLUB HONORS
- UEFA Europe League: 2024

INTERNATIONAL HONORS
- Africa Cup of Nations: runner-up 2023
- FIFA U-20 World Cup: 2017 (England)

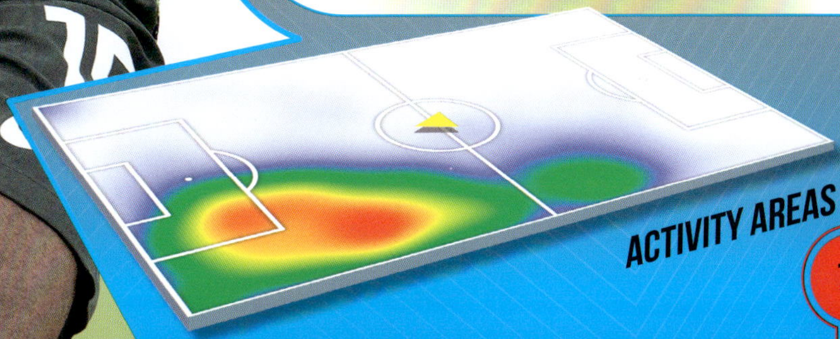

ACTIVITY AREAS

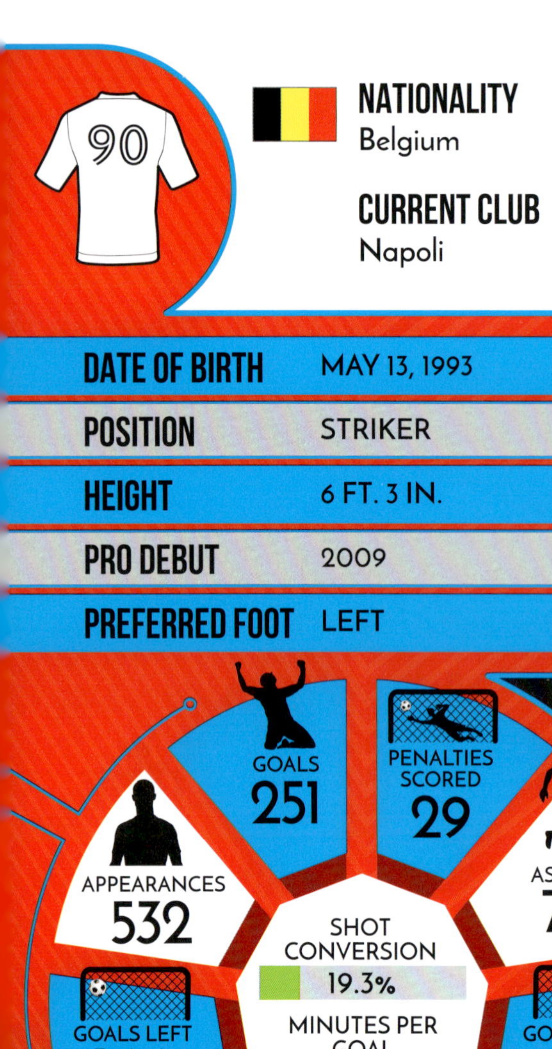

NATIONALITY
Belgium

CURRENT CLUB
Napoli

ROMELU LUKAKU

Romelu Lukaku has a breathtaking pace and dribbling ability. Although he normally plays on the wing, he can also be dangerous in the middle of the park as he can leap high to win headers and shoot powerfully with either foot.

DATE OF BIRTH	MAY 13, 1993
POSITION	STRIKER
HEIGHT	6 FT. 3 IN.
PRO DEBUT	2009
PREFERRED FOOT	LEFT

GOALS 251
PENALTIES SCORED 29
ASSISTS 78
GOALS RIGHT 59
SHOTS 1,298
HEADED GOALS 44
HAT-TRICKS 4
GOALS LEFT 144
APPEARANCES 532

SHOT CONVERSION 19.3%
MINUTES PER GOAL 159

MAJOR CLUB HONORS
⚽ Serie A: 2021 (Inter Milan), 2025 ⚽ UEFA Champions League: runner-up 2023 (Inter Milan) ⚽ Coppa Italia: 2023 (Inter Milan) ⚽ FIFA Club World Cup: 2021 (Chelsea) ⚽ UEFA Europa League: runner-up 2020 (Chelsea)

INTERNATIONAL HONORS
⚽ FIFA World Cup: third place 2018

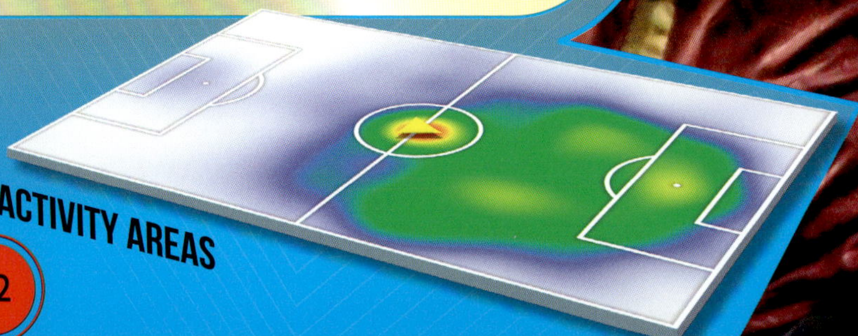

ACTIVITY AREAS

KYLIAN MBAPPÉ

A FIFA World Cup winner with France at just 18 and a runner-up four years later, Kylian Mbappé is counted among the best strikers in world soccer today. The pacey finisher is a superb ball player who consistently gets on the score sheet and sets up chances for his teammates.

NATIONALITY
France

CURRENT CLUB
Real Madrid

DATE OF BIRTH	DEC 12, 1998
POSITION	STRIKER
HEIGHT	5 FT. 10 IN.
PRO DEBUT	2015
PREFERRED FOOT	RIGHT

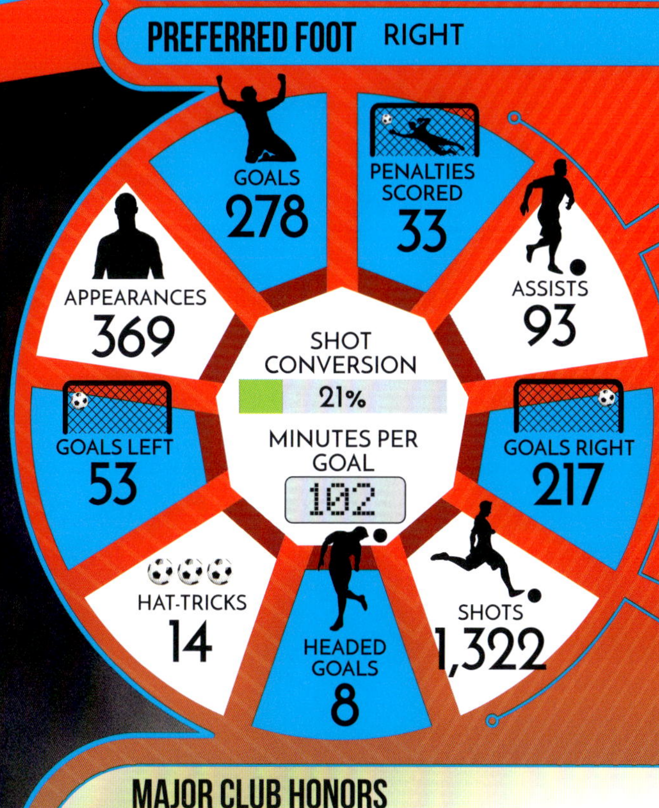

MAJOR CLUB HONORS

⚽ Ligue 1: 2017 (Monaco), 2018, 2019, 2020, 2022, 2023, 2024 (all PSG) ⚽ UEFA Champions League: runner-up 2020 (PSG) ⚽ Coupe de France: 2018, 2020, 2021, 2024 (all PSG) ⚽ FIFA Intercontinental Cup: 2024

INTERNATIONAL HONORS

⚽ FIFA World Cup: 2018, runner-up 2022
⚽ UEFA Nations League: 2021

ACTIVITY AREAS

NATIONALITY
Argentina

CURRENT CLUB
Inter Miami (USA)

LIONEL MESSI

The greatest player of his generation, if not the greatest ever, the 2022 World Cup winner is a fine playmaker with a stunning goal-scoring record. He is also a fantastically fast dribbler who can carve out opportunities to shoot with either foot, from any range, and rarely misses the target.

DATE OF BIRTH	JUN 24, 1987
POSITION	FORWARD
HEIGHT	5 FT. 7 IN.
PRO DEBUT	2003
PREFERRED FOOT	LEFT

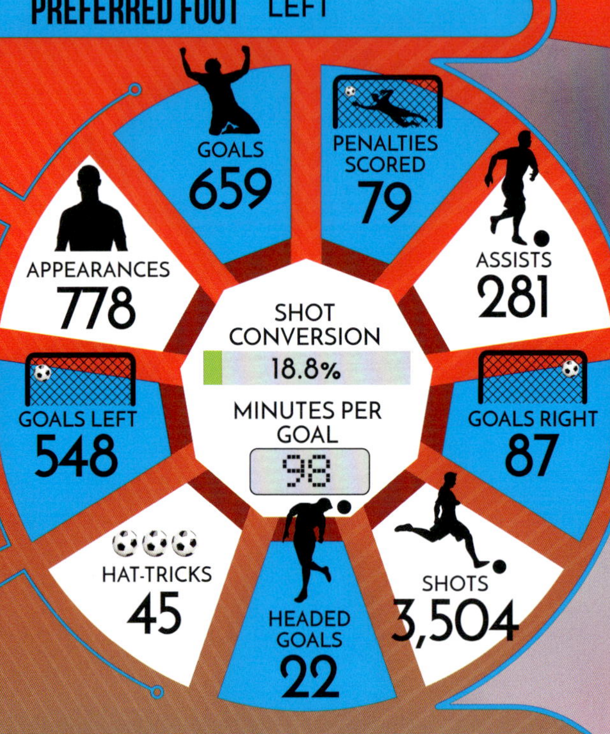

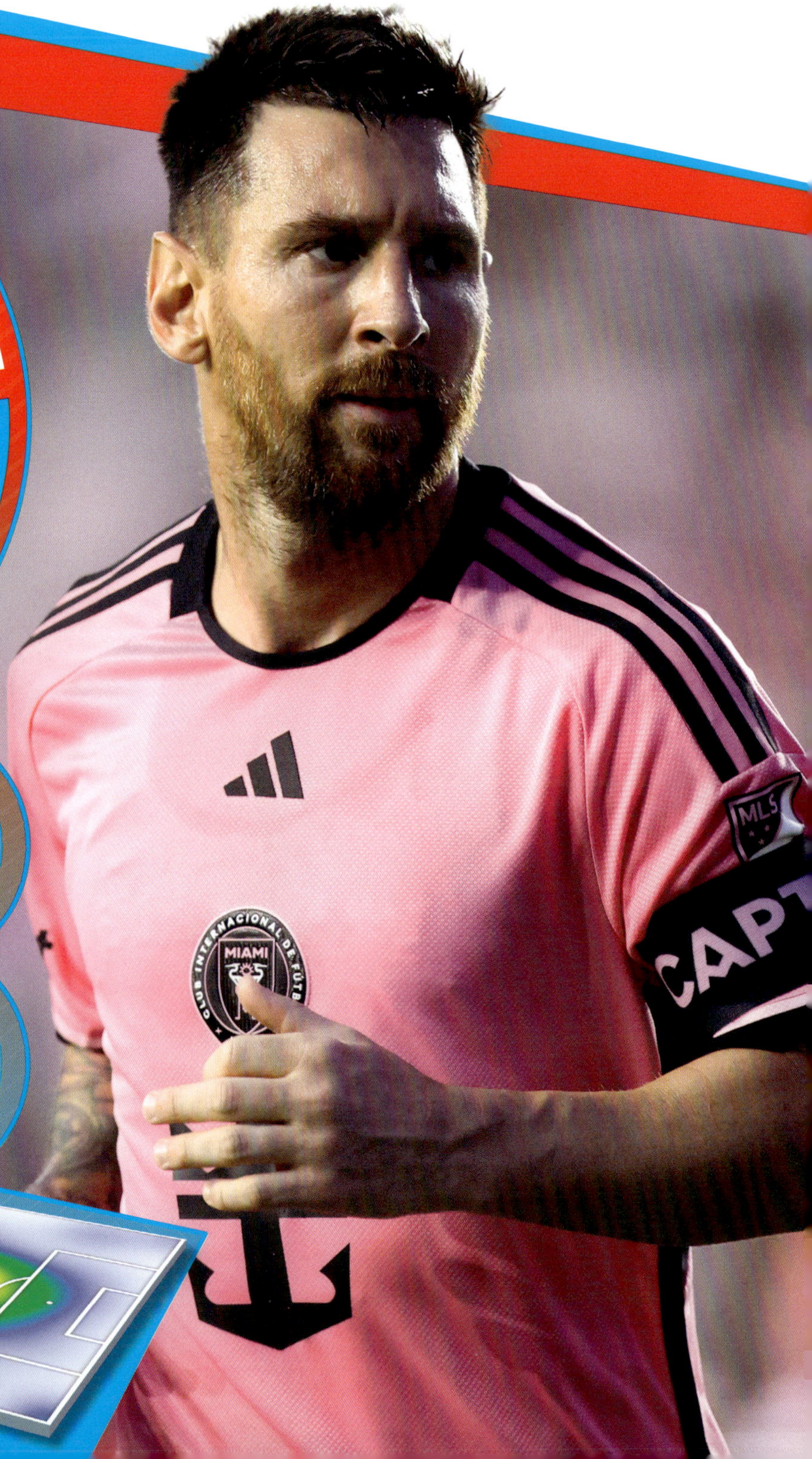

MAJOR CLUB HONORS

⚽ Ligue 1: 2022, 2023 (PSG) ⚽ La Liga: 2005, '06, '09, '10 '11, '13, '15, '16, '18, '19 (all Barça) ⚽ UEFA Champions League: 2006, '09, '11, '15 (all Barça) ⚽ UEFA Super Cup: 2009, '11, '15 (all Barça) ⚽ FIFA Club World Cup: 2009, '11, '15 (all Barça) ⚽ MLS Leagues Cup: 2023

INTERNATIONAL HONORS

- FIFA World Cup: 2022, runner-up 2014
- Olympic Games: gold medal 2008
- Copa América: 2021, 2024, runner-up* 2007*, 2015*, 2016*

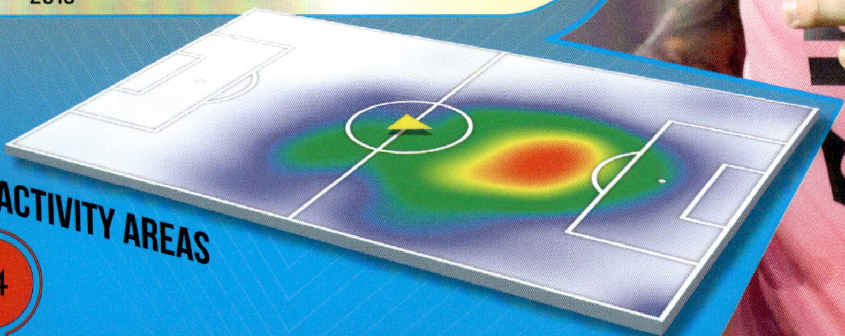

ACTIVITY AREAS

ÁLVARO MORATA

Álvaro Morata is perfectly built for a central striker. Tall, strong, and excellent in the air, he is comfortable with the ball at his feet. Morata is also surprisingly fast and has great tactical and positional awareness.

NATIONALITY
Spain

CURRENT CLUB
AC Milan

DATE OF BIRTH	OCT 23, 1992
POSITION	STRIKER
HEIGHT	6 FT. 2 IN.
PRO DEBUT	2010
PREFERRED FOOT	RIGHT

MAJOR CLUB HONORS

⚽ La Liga: 2012, 2017 (R. Madrid) ⚽ Serie A: 2015, 2016 (all Juventus) ⚽ UEFA Champions League: 2014, '17 (R. Madrid), runner-up 2015 (Juventus) ⚽ UEFA Europa League: 2019 (Chelsea) ⚽ UEFA Super Cup: 2016 (R. Madrid) ⚽ FIFA Club World Cup: 2016 (R. Madrid)

INTERNATIONAL HONORS

- UEFA European Championship: 2024
- UEFA Nations League: 2023, runner-up 2025
- UEFA European U-21 Championship: 2013

ACTIVITY AREAS

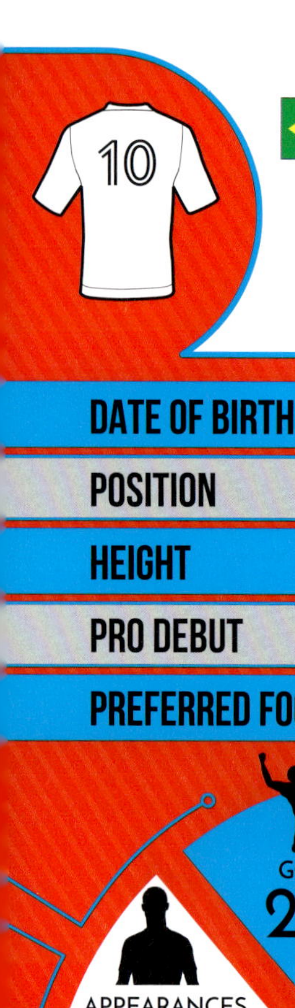

NATIONALITY
Brazil

CURRENT CLUB
Santos (Brazil)

NEYMAR

Neymar's outstanding soccer career has gone full circle and he is back where it all began at Santos in Brazil. He still possesses the pace and phenomenal dribbling to beat defenders in numbers, and can strike fear into the opposition defense with his playmaking skills.

DATE OF BIRTH	FEB 05, 1992
POSITION	FORWARD
HEIGHT	5 FT. 9 IN.
PRO DEBUT	2009
PREFERRED FOOT	RIGHT

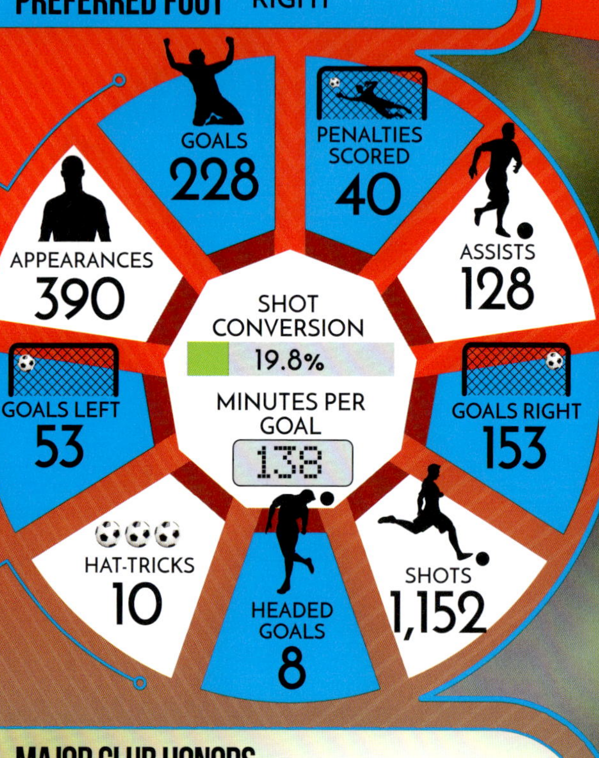

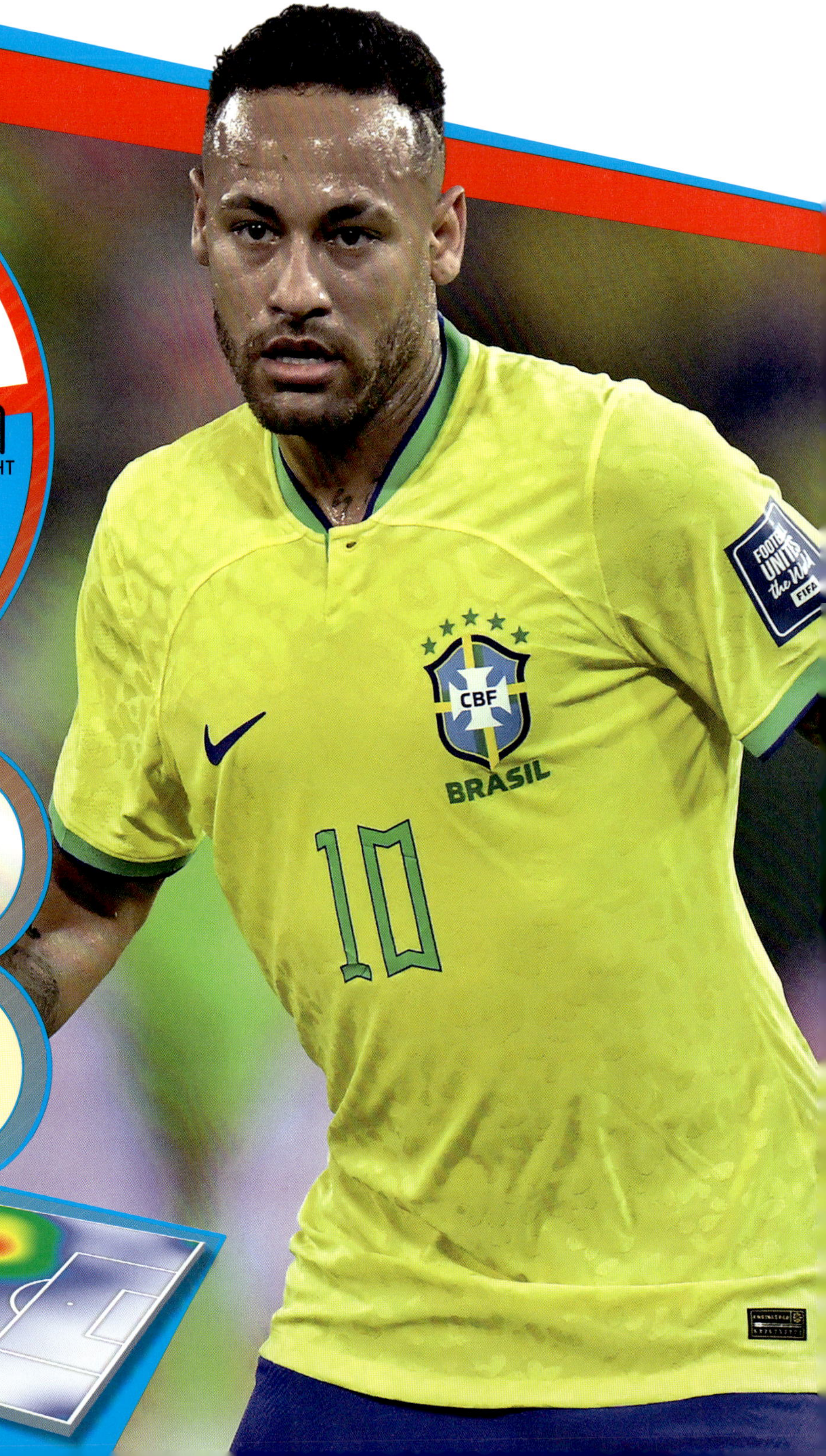

MAJOR CLUB HONORS

⚽ La Liga: 2015, '16, '17 (all Barça) ⚽ Ligue 1: 2018, '19 '20, 2022, 2023 (all PSG) ⚽ UEFA Champions League: 2016 (Barça), runner-up 2020 (PSG) ⚽ FIFA Club World Cup: 2016 (Barça) ⚽ Copa del Rey: 2015, '16, '17 (all Barça) ⚽ Coupe de France: 2018, '20, '21 (all PSG)

INTERNATIONAL HONORS

⚽ Copa América: runner-up 2021
⚽ FIFA Confederations Cup: 2013
⚽ Olympic Games: silver medal 2012, gold medal 2016

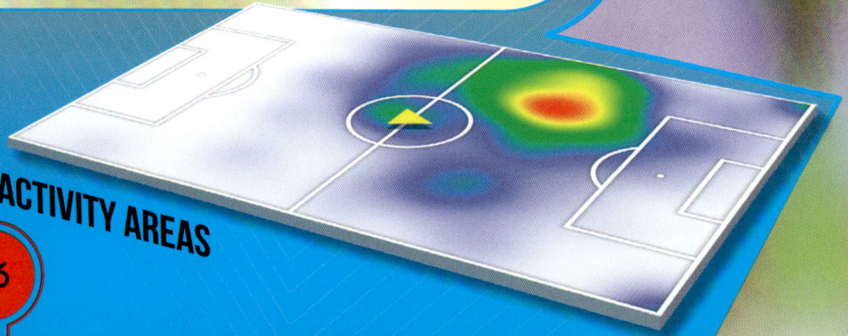

ACTIVITY AREAS

MARCUS RASHFORD

A great player to watch when he is on form, Marcus Rashford has scored some stunning goals for both club and country. He prefers to raid from the left side, to be on his stronger right foot, but his pace and heading ability make him just as dangerous in the middle.

NATIONALITY
England

CURRENT CLUB
Barcelona (on loan)

DATE OF BIRTH	OCT 31, 1997
POSITION	FORWARD
HEIGHT	5 FT. 11 IN.
PRO DEBUT	2015
PREFERRED FOOT	RIGHT

MAJOR CLUB HONORS
- UEFA Europa League: 2017, runner-up 2021 (all Man. United)
- FA Cup: 2016, runner-up 2023, 2024 (all Man. United)
- FA Cup 2016, 2024 (Man. United)

INTERNATIONAL HONORS
- UEFA European Championship: runner-up 2020 (2021)
- UEFA Nations League: third place 2019

ACTIVITY AREAS

NATIONALITY
Portugal

CURRENT CLUB
Al Nassr (S. Arabia)

CRISTIANO RONALDO

The superstar striker has wowed fans across the world with his all-around attacking skills. He is breathtaking to watch when he is running at defenses, brilliant in the air, and a superb finisher with an extraordinary goal-scoring record.

DATE OF BIRTH	FEB 05, 1985
POSITION	FORWARD
HEIGHT	6 FT. 2 IN.
PRO DEBUT	2002
PREFERRED FOOT	RIGHT

GOALS	704
PENALTIES SCORED	139
ASSISTS	189
GOALS RIGHT	470
SHOTS	4,743
HEADED GOALS	111
HAT-TRICKS	53
GOALS LEFT	121
APPEARANCES	820
SHOT CONVERSION	14.8%
MINUTES PER GOAL	99

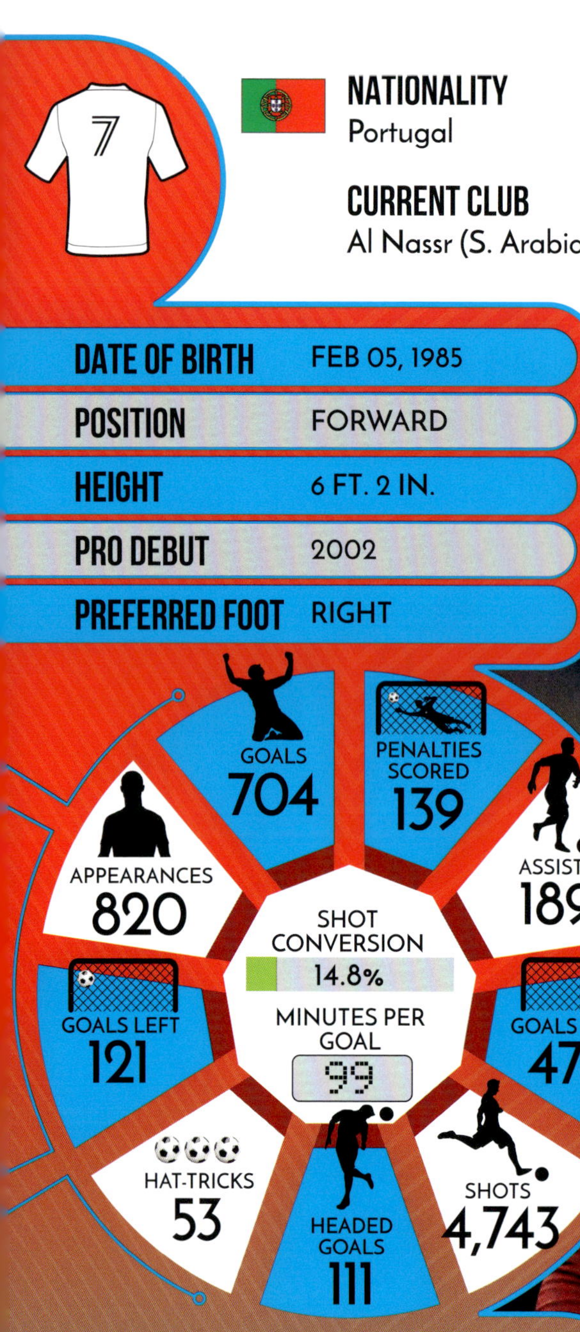

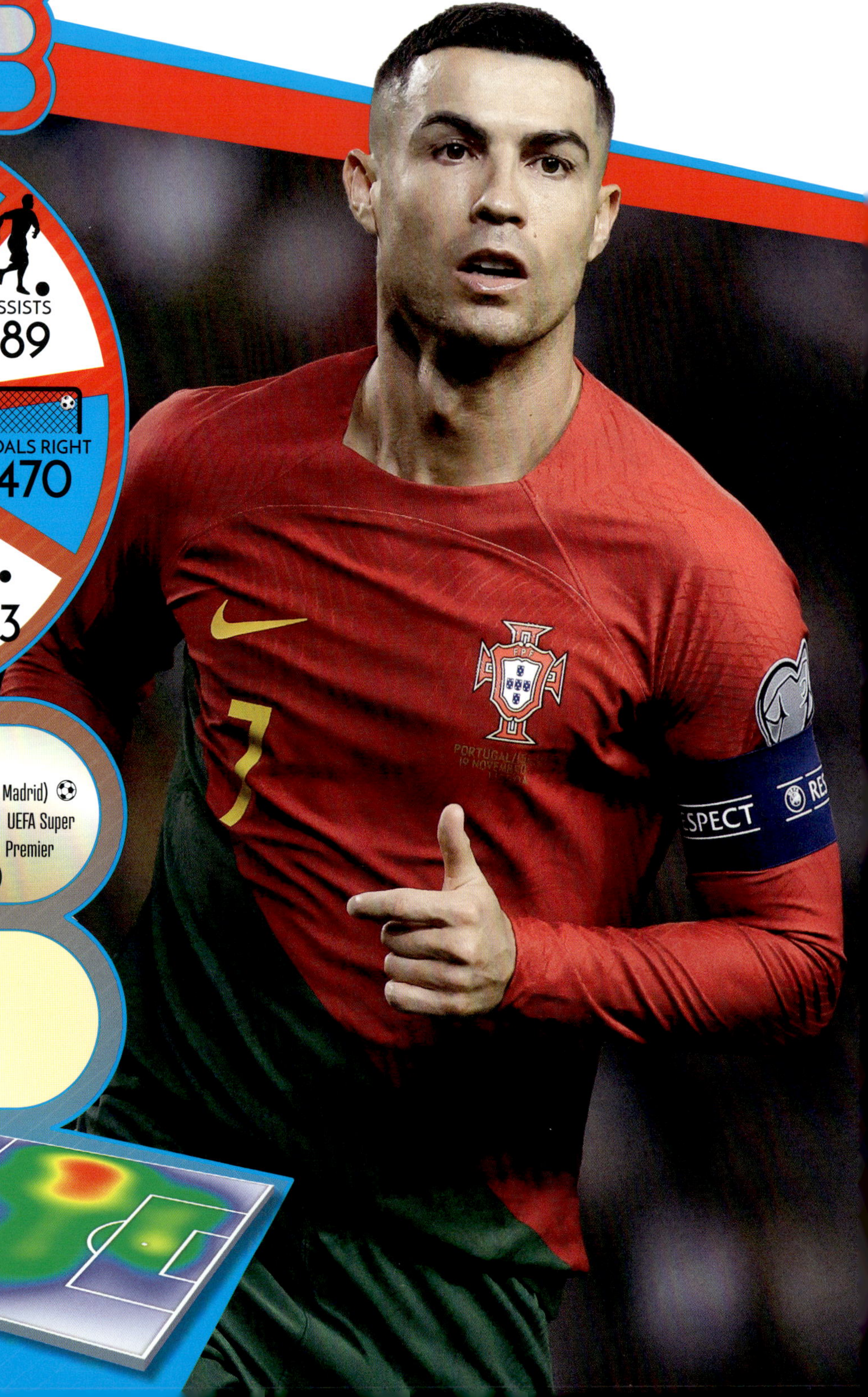

MAJOR CLUB HONORS

⚽ UEFA Champions League: 2008 (Man. U), 2014, '16, '17, '18 (R. Madrid) ⚽ FIFA Club World Cup: 2008 (Man. U), 2014, '16, '17 (R. Madrid) ⚽ UEFA Super Cup: 2014, '17 (R. Madrid) ⚽ Serie A: 2019, '20 (Juventus) ⚽ Premier League: 2007, '08, '09 (Man. U) ⚽ La Liga: 2012, '17 (R. Madrid)

INTERNATIONAL HONORS

⚽ UEFA European Championship: 2016
⚽ UEFA Nations League: 2019, 2025

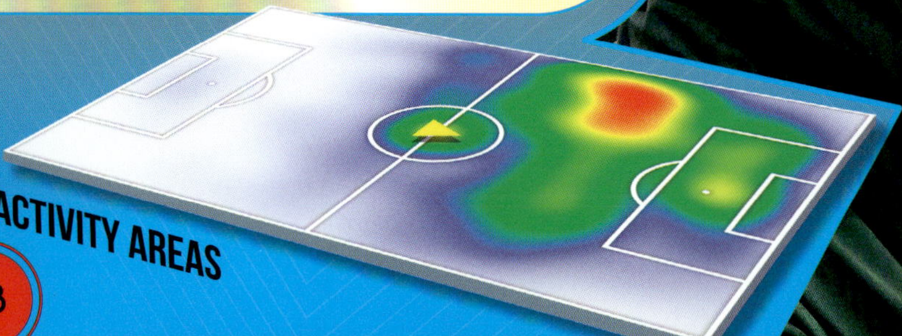

ACTIVITY AREAS

MOHAMED SALAH

The two-time African Footballer Of The Year is a brilliant left-footed attacker who prowls the left wing. Mo Salah has amazing pace with the ability to make angled runs, finding gaps in defenses before scoring spectacular goals.

NATIONALITY
Egypt

CURRENT CLUB
Liverpool

DATE OF BIRTH	JUN 15,1992
POSITION	WINGER
HEIGHT	5 FT. 9 IN.
PRO DEBUT	2010
PREFERRED FOOT	LEFT

GOALS 278

PENALTIES SCORED 42

ASSISTS 132

GOALS RIGHT 41

SHOTS 1,620

HEADED GOALS 10

HAT-TRICKS 6

GOALS LEFT 227

APPEARANCES 508

SHOT CONVERSION 17.2%

MINUTES PER GOAL 145

MAJOR CLUB HONORS

⚽ Premier League: 2020, 2025 ⚽ UEFA Champions League: 2019, runner-up 2018, runner-up 2022 ⚽ UEFA Super Cup: 2019 ⚽ FIFA Club World Cup: 2019 ⚽ FA Cup: 2022

INTERNATIONAL HONORS

⚽ CAF Africa Cup of Nations: runner-up 2017, runner-up 2021

ACTIVITY AREAS

NATIONALITY
South Korea

CURRENT CLUB
Tottenham Hotspur

SON HEUNG-MIN

Son Heung-Min is at his best when he plays behind the main striker. Although excellent with both feet, attacking from the right side is his strength and he converts a lot of chances that are set up by knock-downs or passes across the box.

DATE OF BIRTH	JUL 08, 1992
POSITION	WINGER
HEIGHT	6 FT.
PRO DEBUT	2010
PREFERRED FOOT	BOTH

MAJOR CLUB HONORS
- UEFA Champions League: runner-up 2019
- UEFA Europa League: 2025

INTERNATIONAL HONORS
- AFC Asian Cup: runner-up 2015

ACTIVITY AREAS

VINÍCIUS JÚNIOR

Vinícius Júnior loves terrorizing right-backs, attacking off the left flank, cutting inside to deliver crosses, or shooting with his favored right foot. He brings flair and panache, combined with blistering pace and fantastic dribbling, making him truly world class on his day.

NATIONALITY
Brazil

CURRENT CLUB
Real Madrid

DATE OF BIRTH	JUL 12, 2000
POSITION	WINGER
HEIGHT	5 FT. 9 IN.
PRO DEBUT	2017
PREFERRED FOOT	RIGHT

GOALS 97
PENALTIES SCORED 5
ASSISTS 63
GOALS RIGHT 71
SHOTS 668
HEADED GOALS 5
HAT-TRICKS 3
GOALS LEFT 19
APPEARANCES 313
SHOT CONVERSION 14.5%
MINUTES PER GOAL 216

MAJOR CLUB HONORS

⚽ La Liga: 2020, 2022, 2024 ⚽ UEFA Champions League: 2022, 2024 ⚽ FIFA Club World Cup: 2018, 2022 ⚽ UEFA Super Cup: 2022 ⚽ Copa del Rey: 2023 ⚽ FIFA Intercontinental Cup: 2024

INTERNATIONAL HONORS

⚽ None to date

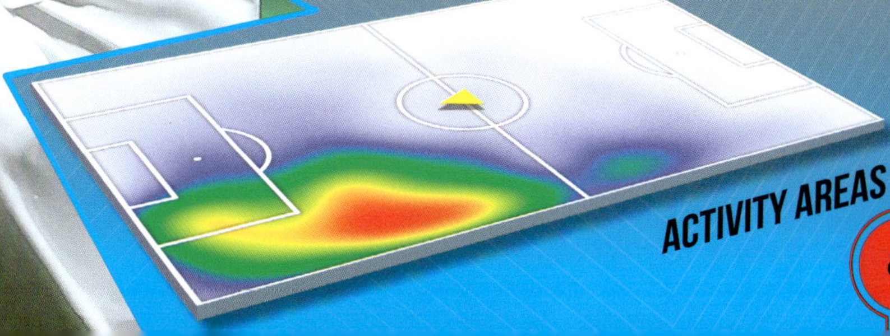

ACTIVITY AREAS

NICO WILLIAMS

Nico Williams is yet another soccer star to come off Spain's production line of talent. Mainly a left-winger, he uses his sublime pace to get past defenders and deliver dangerous crosses, often setting up chances for his older brother Iñaki at Atlético Madrid.

LAMINE YAMAL

Regarded as a prodigy of the modern game, Lamine Yamal is technically gifted, especially with his favored left foot, curling crosses toward the goal. He also plays as a central striker or attacking midfielder, using his pace and control to beat defenders and set up dangerous attacks.

NATIONALITY
Spain

CURRENT CLUB
Barcelona

DATE OF BIRTH	JUL 13, 2007
POSITION	RIGHT-WINGER
HEIGHT	5 FT. 11 IN.
PRO DEBUT	2023
PREFERRED FOOT	LEFT

GOALS 19
PENALTIES SCORED 0
ASSISTS 23
GOALS RIGHT 2
SHOTS 277
HEADED GOALS 0
HAT-TRICKS 0
GOALS LEFT 17
APPEARANCES 96

SHOT CONVERSION 6.9%
MINUTES PER GOAL 355

MAJOR CLUB HONORS
⚽ La Liga 2023, 2025 ⚽ Copa del Rey: 2025

INTERNATIONAL HONORS
⚽ UEFA European Championship: 2024 ⚽ UEFA Nations League: runner-up 2024

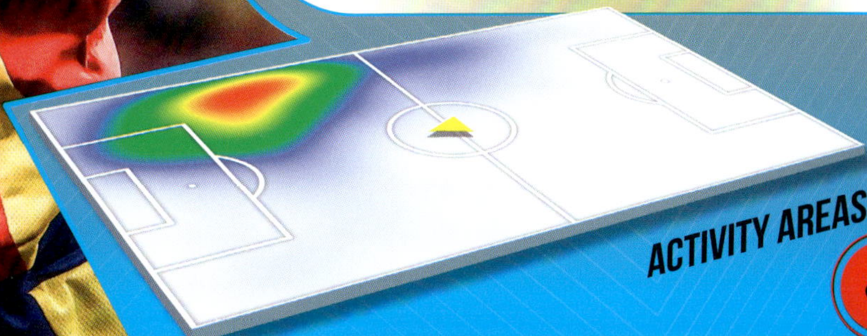

ACTIVITY AREAS

GOALKEEPERS

The goalkeeper is a team's last line of defense and, unlike the other positions, there is no one playing next to them. There is more pressure on goalkeepers than in any other position because when a keeper makes an error, the chances are that the other team will score. The goalies featured in this section are all great shot-stoppers, but some play outside their penalty areas as sweeper-keepers; others have made their reputation as penalty-savers; then there are those who are great at catching the ball or punching it clear.

WHAT DO THE STATS MEAN?

CATCHES

This is the number of times the keeper has dealt with an attack –usually a cross–by catching the ball.

CLEAN SHEETS

Any occasion on which the goalie has not let in a goal for the full duration of the game counts as a clean sheet.

GOALS CONCEDED

This is the number of goals the keeper has conceded in their career in top-division soccer.

PENALTIES FACED/SAVED

This is the number of times a goalie has faced a penalty (excludes shoot-outs) and how successful he has been at saving it.

PUNCHES

This is a measure of how often the keeper has dealt with a dangerous ball (usually a cross) by punching it clear.

SAVES

This shows how many times the goalkeeper has stopped a shot or header that was on target.

Did you know?

Goalkeepers can, in theory, score goals with their hands. If they throw a ball downfield and it goes directly into the opposition net, the goal will count but, of course, the ball would have to travel 90+ yards, which is unlikely.

ALISSON

The Brazilian has proved to be a top keeper at Liverpool. Alisson is a superb shot-stopper and great at dealing with crosses. Incredibly quick off his line to foil any threat, he can turn defense into attack by finding teammates with long or short passes.

NATIONALITY
Brazil

CURRENT CLUB
Liverpool

DATE OF BIRTH	OCT 02, 1992
POSITION	GOALKEEPER
HEIGHT	6 FT. 4 IN.
PRO DEBUT	2013
PREFERRED FOOT	RIGHT

MAJOR CLUB HONORS

- Premier League: 2020, 2025
- UEFA Champions League: 2019, runner-up 2022
- FIFA Club World Cup: 2019
- FA Cup: 2022

INTERNATIONAL HONORS

- Copa América: 2019, runner-up 2021

THIBAUT COURTOIS

Thibaut Courtois uses his height to dominate his penalty area, catching crosses and punching well. An agile shot-stopper, he can get down low to make saves, communicates well with his defense, is excellent coming off his line, and passes well.

NATIONALITY
Belgium

CURRENT CLUB
Real Madrid

DATE OF BIRTH	MAY 11, 1992
POSITION	GOALKEEPER
HEIGHT	6 FT. 6 IN.
PRO DEBUT	2009
PREFERRED FOOT	LEFT

GOALS CONCEDED 502

APPEARANCES 542

PENALTIES SAVED 9

SAVES 1,391

CLEAN SHEETS 225

PENALTIES FACED 51

PUNCHES 157

CATCHES 131

MAJOR CLUB HONORS

⚽ La Liga: 2014 (At. Mad.), 2020, 2022, runner-up 2023, 2024 ⚽ Prem. League: 2015, 2017 (all Chelsea) ⚽ UEFA Champ. League: 2022, 2024 ⚽ UEFA Europa League: 2012 (At. Mad.) ⚽ FIFA Club World Cup: 2018 ⚽ UEFA Super Cup: 2012 (At. Mad.) 2022 ⚽ Copa del Rey: 2013 (At Mad), 2023

INTERNATIONAL HONORS

⚽ FIFA World Cup: third place 2018

ACTIVITY AREAS

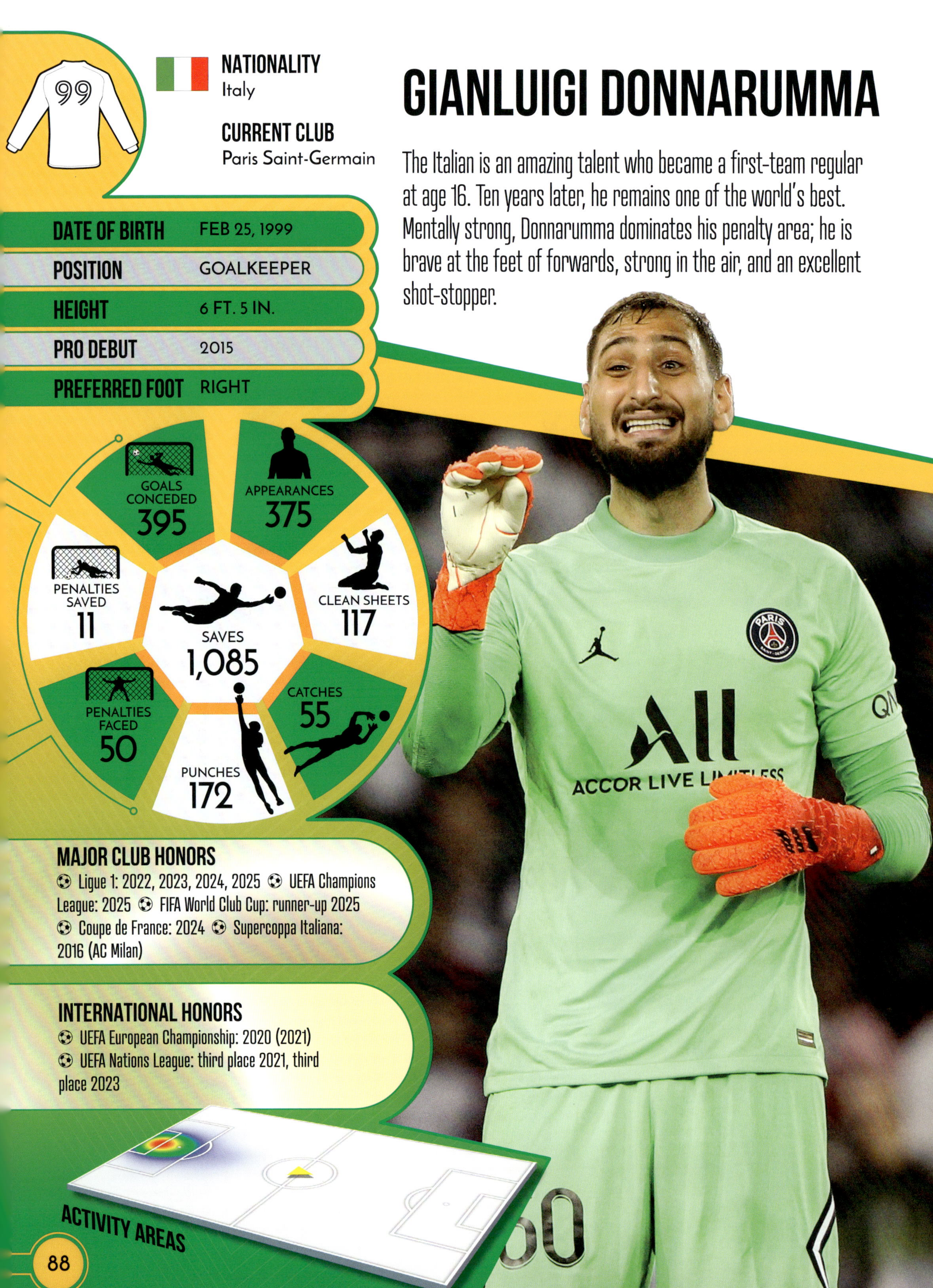

GIANLUIGI DONNARUMMA

The Italian is an amazing talent who became a first-team regular at age 16. Ten years later, he remains one of the world's best. Mentally strong, Donnarumma dominates his penalty area; he is brave at the feet of forwards, strong in the air, and an excellent shot-stopper.

MAJOR CLUB HONORS

⚽ Ligue 1: 2022, 2023, 2024, 2025 ⚽ UEFA Champions League: 2025 ⚽ FIFA World Club Cup: runner-up 2025 ⚽ Coupe de France: 2024 ⚽ Supercoppa Italiana: 2016 (AC Milan)

INTERNATIONAL HONORS

⚽ UEFA European Championship: 2020 (2021)
⚽ UEFA Nations League: third place 2021, third place 2023

EDERSON

Owing to his range of passing and great ball skills, Ederson is often considered a playmaker goalkeeper and counted as one of the best in the English Premier League. He is a fine shot-stopper with a reputation for being a great penalty-kick saver, too.

NATIONALITY
Brazil

CURRENT CLUB
Manchester City

DATE OF BIRTH	AUG 17, 1993
POSITION	GOALKEEPER
HEIGHT	6 FT. 2 IN.
PRO DEBUT	2011
PREFERRED FOOT	LEFT

MAJOR CLUB HONORS
- Premier League: 2018, 2019, 2021, 2022, 2023, 2024
- UEFA Champions League: runner-up 2021, 2023
- FA Cup: 2019, 2023, runner-up 2024, runner-up 2025
- FIFA Club World Cup: 2023

INTERNATIONAL HONORS
- Copa América: 2019, runner-up 2021

ACTIVITY AREAS

PÉTER GULÁCSI

Péter Gulácsi is dedicated to preparing for every soccer situation he faces. He studies approaching forwards to get an instinct for where they are going to shoot, gets into the right position, and then makes difficult saves look very easy.

DATE OF BIRTH	MAY 06, 1990
POSITION	GOALKEEPER
HEIGHT	6 FT. 3 IN.
PRO DEBUT	2008
PREFERRED FOOT	RIGHT

MAJOR CLUB HONORS

- Austrian Bundesliga: 2014, 2015 (Red Bull Salzburg)
- Austrian Cup: 2014, 2015 (Red Bull Salzburg)
- DFB-Pokal: runner-up 2019, runner-up 2021*, 2022, 2023

INTERNATIONAL HONORS

- FIFA U-20 World Cup: third place 2009

LUKAS HRADECKY

Like many goalkeepers, it wasn't until his thirties that Lukas Hradecky reached his peak. He is an excellent shot-stopper with plenty of confidence, decisive when dealing with crosses, and brilliant at organizing his penalty area and communicating with defenders.

NATIONALITY
Finland

CURRENT CLUB
Bayer Leverkusen

DATE OF BIRTH	NOV 24, 1989
POSITION	GOALKEEPER
HEIGHT	6 FT. 4 IN.
PRO DEBUT	2008
PREFERRED FOOT	RIGHT

MAJOR CLUB HONORS
- Bundesliga: 2024
- DFB Pokal: 2018 (Eintracht Frankfurt), 2024
- UEFA Europa League: runner-up 2024

INTERNATIONAL HONORS
- Baltic Cup: Runner-up 2012

ACTIVITY AREAS

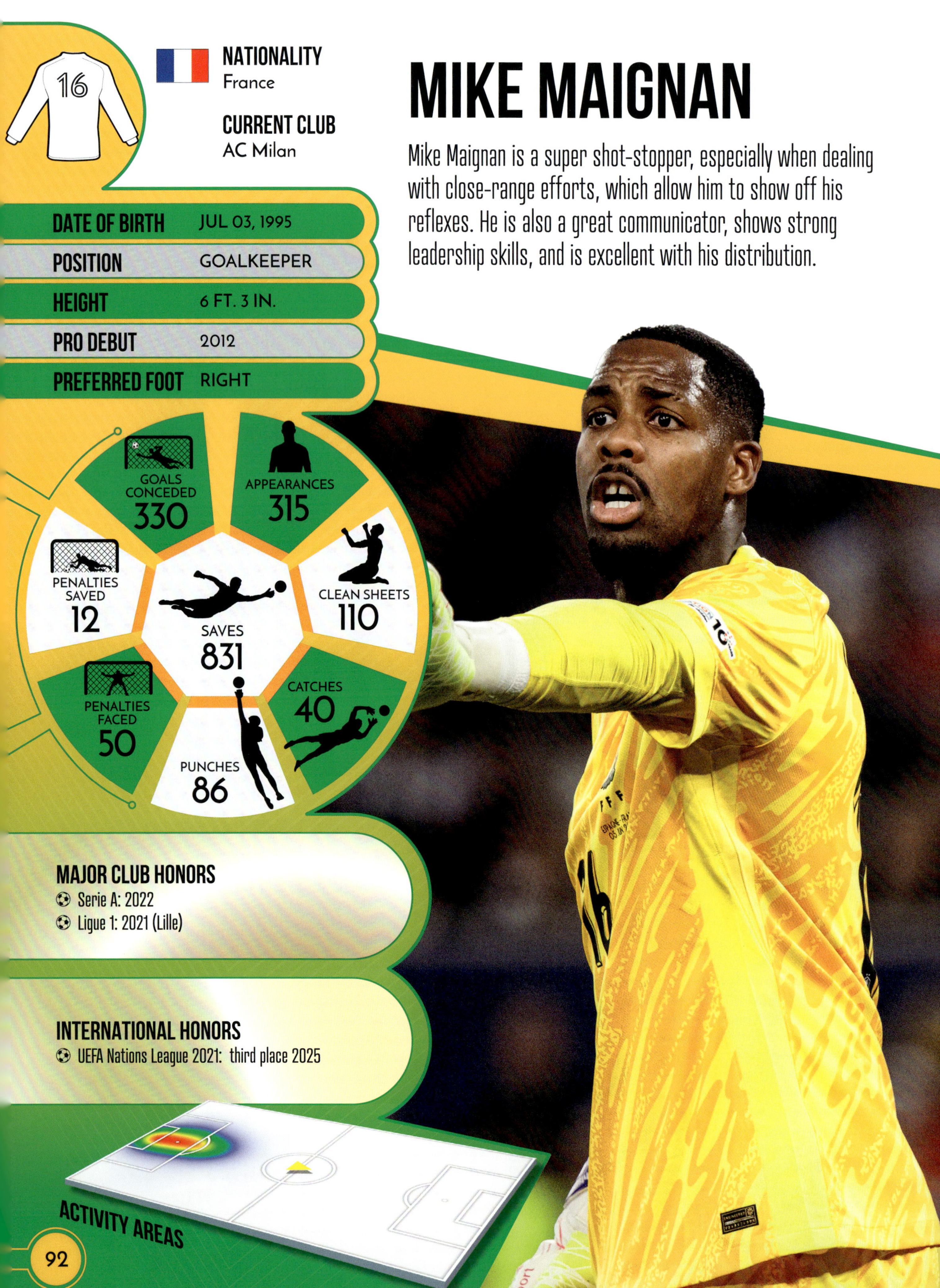

MIKE MAIGNAN

16

NATIONALITY
France

CURRENT CLUB
AC Milan

Mike Maignan is a super shot-stopper, especially when dealing with close-range efforts, which allow him to show off his reflexes. He is also a great communicator, shows strong leadership skills, and is excellent with his distribution.

DATE OF BIRTH	JUL 03, 1995
POSITION	GOALKEEPER
HEIGHT	6 FT. 3 IN.
PRO DEBUT	2012
PREFERRED FOOT	RIGHT

GOALS CONCEDED 330
APPEARANCES 315
PENALTIES SAVED 12
SAVES 831
CLEAN SHEETS 110
PENALTIES FACED 50
CATCHES 40
PUNCHES 86

MAJOR CLUB HONORS
- Serie A: 2022
- Ligue 1: 2021 (Lille)

INTERNATIONAL HONORS
- UEFA Nations League 2021: third place 2025

ACTIVITY AREAS

EMILIANO MARTÍNEZ

An immensely athletic goalkeeper, Emiliano Martínez is capable of reaching shots going into the top corner with either hand. His quick feet mean he gets into good positions not only to make saves but also reduce the angle for shots.

NATIONALITY
Argentina

CURRENT CLUB
TBC

DATE OF BIRTH	SEP 02, 1992
POSITION	GOALKEEPER
HEIGHT	6 FT. 5 IN.
PRO DEBUT	2012
PREFERRED FOOT	RIGHT

MAJOR CLUB HONORS

- FA Cup: 2020 (Arsenal)

INTERNATIONAL HONORS

- Copa América: 2021, 2024
- FIFA World Cup: 2022
- CONMEBOL-UEFA Cup of Champions: 2022

ACTIVITY AREAS

KEYLOR NAVAS

Keylor Navas is strong, athletic, and a fine organzser and shot stopper. Part of the new breed of hyper-aggressive keepers, he has the confidence to play off his lines, even in situations that might call for more restrained positioning. Navas left French club PSG in 2024 after five years.

MAJOR CLUB HONORS

⚽ Ligue 1: 2020, '22, '24 (all PSG) ⚽ La Liga: 2017 (R. Madrid) ⚽ UEFA Champions League: 2016, '17, '18 (all R. Mad.) runner-up 2020 (PSG) ⚽ FIFA World Club Cup: 2014, '16, '17, '18 (all R. Mad.) ⚽ UEFA Super Cup: 2017 (R. Mad.) ⚽ Coupe de France: 2020, '21, '24 (all PSG)

INTERNATIONAL HONORS

⚽ UNCAF Nations Cup: runner-up 2009, runner-up 2011

MANUEL NEUER

A top-level keeper for more than 20 years, Manuel Neuer redefined the way goalkeepers play the position, being the original "sweeper-keeper." A great distributor, he commands his penalty area and excels as a shot-stopper and organizer.

NATIONALITY
Germany

CURRENT CLUB
Bayern Munich

DATE OF BIRTH	MAR 27, 1986
POSITION	GOALKEEPER
HEIGHT	6 FT. 4 IN.
PRO DEBUT	2004
PREFERRED FOOT	RIGHT

MAJOR CLUB HONORS

⚽ Bundesliga: 2013, 2014, 2015, 2016, 2017, 2018, 2019, 2020, 2021, 2022, 2023, 2025 ⚽ UEFA Champions League: 2013, 2020 ⚽ UEFA Super Cup: 2013, 2020 ⚽ FIFA Club World Cup: 2013, 2020 ⚽ DFB-Pokal 2011 (Schalke 04), 2013, 2014, 2016 2019, 2020

INTERNATIONAL HONORS

⚽ FIFA World Cup: 2014, third place 2010

ACTIVITY AREAS

JAN OBLAK

One of the world's most agile and accomplished keepers, Jan Oblak is blessed with the quick reflexes to be able to come off his line to snuff out any signs of danger. His communication skills make him adept at organizing his defense and taking on the role of team vice-captain.

MAJOR CLUB HONORS

- La Liga: 2021
- UEFA Champions League: runner-up 2016
- UEFA Europa League: 2018
- UEFA Super Cup: 2018

INTERNATIONAL HONORS

- None to date

RUI PATRÍCIO

Rui Patrício is an old-fashioned continental goalkeeper, primarily a shot-stopper who allows his defenders to deal with crosses into the danger area. He is an expert at coming off his line to narrow angles. Coming to the end of his career, in late May 2025, Patrício signed a short-term deal with UAE Pro League side Al Ain.

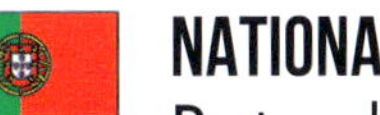

NATIONALITY
Portugal

CURRENT CLUB
Al Ain (UAE)

DATE OF BIRTH	FEB 15, 1988
POSITION	GOALKEEPER
HEIGHT	6 FT. 3 IN.
PRO DEBUT	2006
PREFERRED FOOT	LEFT

GOALS CONCEDED 379

APPEARANCES 319

PENALTIES SAVED 6

SAVES 816

CLEAN SHEETS 99

PENALTIES FACED 37

PUNCHES 61

CATCHES 79

MAJOR CLUB HONORS

- Europa Conference League: 2022 (Roma)
- UEFA Europa League: runner-up 2023
- Taça de Portugal: 2007, 2008, 2015 (Sporting Clube)

INTERNATIONAL HONORS

- UEFA European Championship: 2016
- UEFA Nations League: 2019

ACTIVITY AREAS

JORDAN PICKFORD

Playing for one of the lesser teams in the English Premier League, Jordan Pickford is kept busy and is an excellent shot-stopper. Not the tallest of goalkeepers, he prefers to punch rather than catch the ball and is also very good at distributing to teammates to initiate attacks.

DATE OF BIRTH	MAR 07, 1994
POSITION	GOALKEEPER
HEIGHT	6 FT. 1 IN.
PRO DEBUT	2011
PREFERRED FOOT	LEFT

MAJOR CLUB HONORS

- None to date

INTERNATIONAL HONORS

- UEFA European Championship: runner-up 2020, runner-up 2024
- UEFA Natiom League: third place 2019

DAVID RAYA

David Raya dominates his penalty area, not only in dealing with crosses, but also his improved technique on the ball allows his defenders to play higher up the field. He has fine anticipation and is a top shot-stopper, too.

NATIONALITY
Spain

CURRENT CLUB
Arsenal

DATE OF BIRTH	SEP 15, 1995
POSITION	GOALKEEPER
HEIGHT	6 FT.
PRO DEBUT	2014
PREFERRED FOOT	RIGHT

GOALS CONCEDED
147

APPEARANCES
154

PENALTIES SAVED
3

SAVES
413

CLEAN SHEETS
59

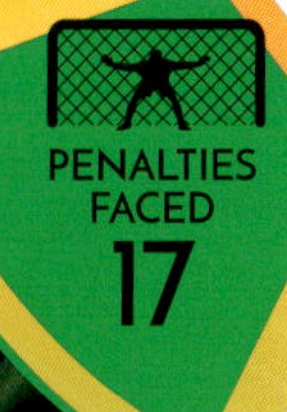
PENALTIES FACED
17

PUNCHES
36

CATCHES
30

MAJOR CLUB HONORS

- Premier League: runner-up 2024, runner-up 2025

INTERNATIONAL HONORS

- UEFA European Championship: 2024
- UEFA Nations League: 2023 runner-up 2025

ACTIVITY AREAS

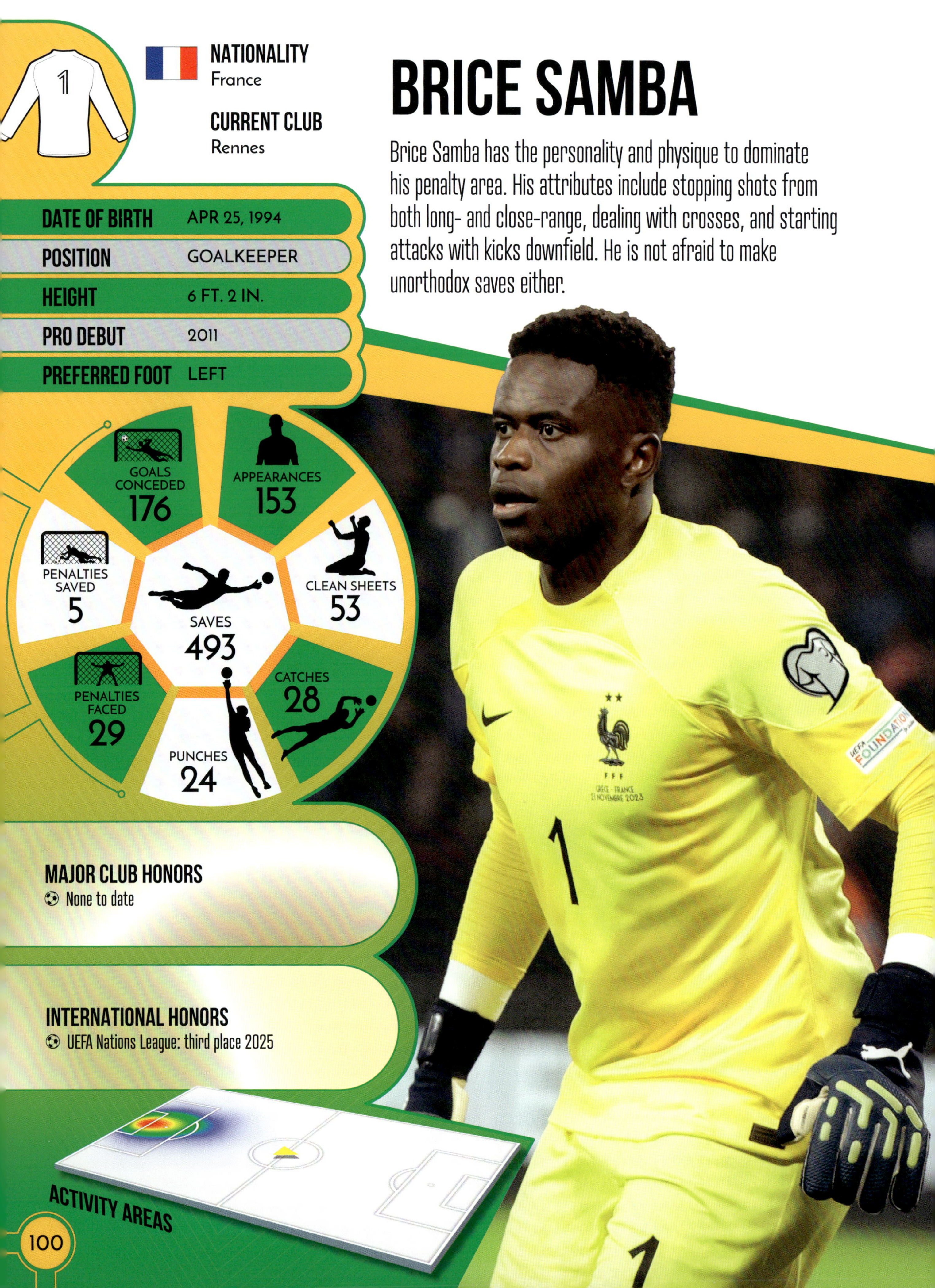

BRICE SAMBA

NATIONALITY
France

CURRENT CLUB
Rennes

Brice Samba has the personality and physique to dominate his penalty area. His attributes include stopping shots from both long- and close-range, dealing with crosses, and starting attacks with kicks downfield. He is not afraid to make unorthodox saves either.

DATE OF BIRTH	APR 25, 1994
POSITION	GOALKEEPER
HEIGHT	6 FT. 2 IN.
PRO DEBUT	2011
PREFERRED FOOT	LEFT

GOALS CONCEDED 176
APPEARANCES 153
PENALTIES SAVED 5
SAVES 493
CLEAN SHEETS 53
PENALTIES FACED 29
CATCHES 28
PUNCHES 24

MAJOR CLUB HONORS
- None to date

INTERNATIONAL HONORS
- UEFA Nations League: third place 2025

ACTIVITY AREAS

ROBERT SÁNCHEZ

Robert Sánchez is an agile shot-stopper who also is excellent at communicating with his back four to help play the ball out of defense. He has the unique ability to leave it until the last moment to come off his line, making it more difficult for opponents to get the shot past him.

NATIONALITY
Spain

CURRENT CLUB
Chelsea

DATE OF BIRTH	NOV 18, 1997
POSITION	GOALKEEPER
HEIGHT	6 FT. 5 IN.
PRO DEBUT	2018
PREFERRED FOOT	RIGHT

GOALS CONCEDED 159
APPEARANCES 136
PENALTIES SAVED 3
SAVES 364
CLEAN SHEETS 40
PENALTIES FACED 21
PUNCHES 33
CATCHES 16

MAJOR CLUB HONORS
- FIFA World Club Cup: 2025
- UEFA Conference League: 2025
- EFL Cup: runner-up: 2024

INTERNATIONAL HONORS
- UEFA Nations League: runner-up 2021

ACTIVITY AREAS

YANN SOMMER

Yann Sommer is not tall for a goalkeeper but he has great anticipation, reflexes, and footwork, which more than make up for his lack of height. A good shot-stopper, he is very comfortable playing as a sweeper-keeper, too.

NATIONALITY
Switzerland

CURRENT CLUB
Inter Milan

DATE OF BIRTH	DEC 17, 1988
POSITION	GOALKEEPER
HEIGHT	6 FT.
PRO DEBUT	2005
PREFERRED FOOT	LEFT

MAJOR CLUB HONORS

⚽ Serie A: 2024 ⚽ UEFA Champions League: runner-up 2025 ⚽ Bundesliga: 2023 (Bayern Munich)

INTERNATIONAL HONORS

⚽ None to date

WOJCIECH SZCZĘSNY

Wojciech Szczęsny has grown into one of Europe's most consistent keepers. A natural shot-stopper with lightning reflexes, he is also great at controlling his penalty area, dealing with crosses, and setting up counterattacks with quick clearances.

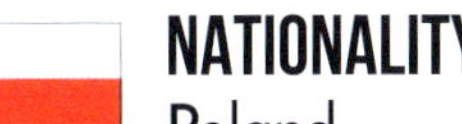

NATIONALITY
Poland

CURRENT CLUB
Barcelona

DATE OF BIRTH	APR 18, 1990
POSITION	GOALKEEPER
HEIGHT	6 FT. 5 IN.
PRO DEBUT	2009
PREFERRED FOOT	RIGHT

GOALS CONCEDED 526

APPEARANCES 503

PENALTIES SAVED 16

SAVES 1,307

CLEAN SHEETS 183

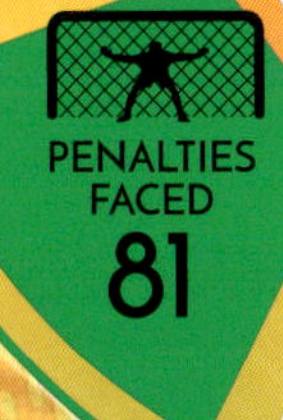

PENALTIES FACED 81

PUNCHES 197

CATCHES 208

MAJOR CLUB HONORS

⚽ La Liga: 2025 ⚽ Serie A: 2018, 2019, 2020 (all Juventus) ⚽ Copa del Rey: 2025 ⚽ FA Cup: 2014, 2015 (all Arsenal) ⚽ Coppa Italia: 2018, 2021, 2024 (all Juventus) ⚽

INTERNATIONAL HONORS

⚽ None to date

ACTIVITY AREAS

MANAGERS

Head coaches are as different from each other as players who play in different positions. But the majority of the 12 featured in this section have one thing in common: they are all winners, either in their domestic leagues or in continental competitions. Some, such as Mikel Arteta, were successful players themselves and trophy winners well before they entered management, while others, such as Claudio Ranieri, had less fruitful playing careers but have had great success as the brains behind a top team.

WHAT DO THE STATS MEAN?

GAMES MANAGED

This is the number of games the coach has been in charge of across their entire career in soccer management.

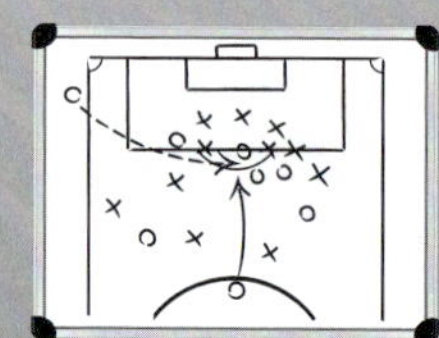

TEAMS MANAGED

The number of clubs (first teams only) that the coach has managed during their career to date.

WINS

This is the number of games the coach has won, including one leg of a cup-tie, even if the tie was lost on aggregate or penalties.

TROPHIES

The trophy list features the head coach's success in domestic top divisions, national and league cups, and international club competitions, except any super cups.

Did you know?

Eddie Howe coached Premier League team Newcastle United to their first domestic cup win for 70 years and first of any type for 56 years. He was also the first English manager in 17 years to win a domestic trophy.

XABI ALONSO

NATIONALITY
Spain

CURRENT CLUB
Real Madrid

Xabi Alonso is Europe's most in-demand coach after winning the Bundesliga title in his first full season. His teams play 3–4–2–1 formation, inviting pressure, then counterattacking and taking advantage of holes in the opposition's defenses.

YEARS AS HEAD COACH: 6

FIRST CLUB: REAL SOCIEDAD B

CLUBS MANAGED	GAMES	LEAGUE TITLES
2	237	1
WINS	**DRAW**	**LOSSES**
127	56	54
CHAMPIONS LEAGUE TROPHIES	**EUROPA LEAGUE TROPHIES**	**OTHER TROPHIES***
0	0	2

*Excludes Super Cups

MAJOR CLUB HONORS

- Bundesliga: 2024 (Bayer Leverkusen)
- DFB-Pokal: 2024 (Bayer Leverkusen)
- UEFA Europa League: runner-up 2024 (Bayer Leverkusen)

CARLO ANCELOTTI

NATIONALITY
Italy

CURRENT TEAM
Brazil

The vastly experienced and accomplished Carlo Ancelotti uses different systems depending on the opposition and players available. His favorite formation is 4–4–2, sometimes in a diamond, other times with four midfielders in a line across the field.

YEARS AS HEAD COACH : 30

FIRST CLUB: REGGIANA

CLUBS MANAGED	GAMES	LEAGUE TITLES
10	1,401	6
WINS	**DRAW**	**LOSSES**
838	306	257
CHAMPIONS LEAGUE TROPHIES	**EUROPA LEAGUE TROPHIES**	**OTHER TROPHIES***
5	0	19

*Excludes Super Cups

MAJOR CLUB HONORS

- La Liga: 2022, runner-up 2023, 2024 (all Real Madrid)
- UEFA Champions League: 2003, 2007 (all AC Milan), 2014, 2022, 2024 (all Real Madrid
- FIFA Club World Cup: 2007 (AC Milan), 2014, 2022 (all Real Madrid
- Serie A: 2004 (AC Milan)
- Premier League: 2010 (Chelsea)
- Ligue 1: 2013 (Paris St-Germain)
- Copa del Rey: 2014, 2023 (all R. Mad.)
- Coppa Italia: 2003 (AC Milan)
- Bundesliga: 2017 (Bayern Munich)

MIKEL ARTETA

NATIONALITY
Spain

CURRENT CLUB
Arsenal

Mikel Arteta gambled on taking a high-profile club as his first job in management. He changed his style from a defensively strong 5–4–1 to a more aggressive attacking 4–2–3–1, with players causing danger from anywhere on the field.

YEARS AS HEAD COACH: 6

FIRST CLUB: ARSENAL

CLUBS MANAGED	GAMES	LEAGUE TITLES
1	290	0
WINS	**DRAW**	**LOSSES**
169	55	66
CHAMPIONS LEAGUE TROPHIES	**EUROPA LEAGUE TROPHIES**	**OTHER TROPHIES***
0	0	3

*Excludes Super Cups

MAJOR CLUB HONORS
- Premier League: runner-up 2023, runner-up 2024, runner-up 2025
- FA Cup: 2020
- FA Community Shield: 2020, 2023

UNAI EMERY

NATIONALITY
Spain

CURRENT CLUB
Aston Villa

Unai Emery has enjoyed great success managing clubs that have a modest budget. His preference is either a 4–2–3–1 formation or 4–4–2, the choice dependent on the attacking skills of the two central midfielders and their ability to retain possession.

YEARS AS HEAD COACH: 21

FIRST CLUB: LORCA DEPORTIVA

CLUBS MANAGED	GAMES	LEAGUE TITLES
9	1,066	1
WINS	**DRAW**	**LOSSES**
569	231	266
CHAMPIONS LEAGUE TROPHIES	**EUROPA LEAGUE TROPHIES**	**OTHER TROPHIES***
0	4	6

*Excludes Super Cups

MAJOR CLUB HONORS
- UEFA Europa League: 2014, 2015, 2016 (all Sevilla), 2021 (Villareal), runner-up 2019 (Arsenal)
- Ligue 1: 2018 (Paris Saint-Germain)
- Coupe de France: 2017, 2018 (all Paris Saint-Germain)

LUIS ENRIQUE

NATIONALITY
Spain

CURRENT CLUB
Paris Saint-Germain

Luis Enrique will not compromise his soccer beliefs, and he will play in the formation that suits his available players, normally 4–3–3 or 3–4–3. He wants his players to express themselves on the ball whenever possible.

YEARS AS HEAD COACH: 14

FIRST CLUB: BARCELONA B

CLUBS MANAGED	GAMES	LEAGUE TITLES
5	498	4
WINS	**DRAW**	**LOSSES**
306	98	94
CHAMPIONS LEAGUE TROPHIES	**EUROPA LEAGUE TROPHIES**	**OTHER TROPHIES***
2	0	9

*Excludes Super Cups

MAJOR CLUB HONORS

- UEFA Champions League; 2015 (Barcelona), 2025
- Ligue 1: 2024, 2025
- La Liga; 2015, 2016 (all Barcelona)
- FIFA World Club Cup; 2015 (Barcelona), runner-up 2025
- Coupe de France: 2024, 2025
- Copa del Rey; 2015, 2016, 2017 (all Barcelona)

HANSI FLICK

NATIONALITY
Germany

CURRENT CLUB
Barcelona

Hansi Flick won many medals and trophies as a player, then as assistant coach and head coach at Bayern Munich. He's also managed the German national team. His teams focus on playing high-pressing, attacking soccer.

YEARS AS HEAD COACH: 29

FIRST CLUB: VICTORIA BAMMENTAL

CLUBS MANAGED	GAMES	LEAGUE TITLES
4	146	3
WINS	**DRAW**	**LOSSES**
114	16	16
CHAMPIONS LEAGUE TROPHIES	**EUROPA LEAGUE TROPHIES**	**OTHER TROPHIES***
1	0	6

*Excludes Super Cups

MAJOR CLUB HONORS

- La Liga: 2025
- Bundesliga: 2020, 2021 all (Bayern Munich)
- UEFA Champions League: 2020 (Bayern Munich)
- Copa del Rey: 2025
- DFB-Pokal: 2020 (Bayern Munich)
- FIFA Club World Cup: 2020 (Bayern Munich)
- UEFA Super Cup: 2020 (Bayern Munich)

GIAN PIERO GASPERINI

NATIONALITY
Italy

CURRENT CLUB
Roma

Gian Piero Gasperini wants his teams to be attacking, but to defend man-for-man when not in possession. His 3–4–3 formation is fluid; when his teams attack, the wing-backs play as wide midfielders and try to outnumber opposing defenders.

YEARS AS HEAD COACH: 22

FIRST CLUB: CROTONE

CLUBS MANAGED	GAMES	LEAGUE TITLES
5	874	0
WINS	**DRAW**	**LOSSES**
402	209	263
CHAMPIONS LEAGUE TROPHIES	**EUROPA LEAGUE TROPHIES**	**OTHER TROPHIES***
0	1	0

*Excludes Super Cups

MAJOR CLUB HONORS

- UEFA Europa League: 2024

PEP GUARDIOLA

NATIONALITY
Spain

CURRENT CLUB
Manchester City

Once a great midfielder himself, Pep Guardiola devised the *tika-taka* passing system at Barcelona (from 2008 to '12). Disciplined in possession, without the ball his teams press the opposition into making mistakes and then launch rapid counterattacks.

YEARS AS HEAD COACH: 17

FIRST CLUB: BARCELONA B

CLUBS MANAGED	GAMES	LEAGUE TITLES
4	979	12
WINS	**DRAW**	**LOSSES**
701	154	124
CHAMPIONS LEAGUE TROPHIES	**EUROPA LEAGUE TROPHIES**	**OTHER TROPHIES***
3	0	24

*Excludes Super Cups

MAJOR CLUB HONORS

- Premier League: 2018, 2019, 2021, 2022, 2023, 2024
- UEFA Champions League: 2009, 2011 Barcelona), runner-up 2021, 2023
- FIFA Club World Cup: 2009, 2011 (Barcelona), 2013 (B. Munich)
- La Liga: 2009, 2010, 2011 (Barcelona)
- Bundesliga: 2014, 2015, 2016 (B. Munich)
- FA Cup: 2019, 2023, Runner-up 2024, runner-up 2025

EDDIE HOWE

NATIONALITY
England

CURRENT CLUB
Newcastle United

Eddie Howe's reputation has improved dramatically, and he is now considered an elite head coach. He prefers a 4–3–3 formation in possession, and 4–5–1 without the ball, stressing pressure on the opposing defenders, to force quick turnovers.

YEARS AS HEAD COACH: 17

FIRST CLUB: AFC BOURNEMOUTH

CLUBS MANAGED	GAMES	LEAGUE TITLES
3	718	0
WINS	**DRAW**	**LOSSES**
316	151	251
CHAMPIONS LEAGUE TROPHIES	**EUROPA LEAGUE TROPHIES**	**OTHER TROPHIES***
0	0	1

*Excludes Super Cups

MAJOR CLUB HONORS

- EFL Cup: runner-up 2023, 2025

SIMONE INZAGHI

NATIONALITY
Italy

CURRENT CLUB
Al Hillal (Saudi Arabia)

Simone Inzaghi's teams almost always play in a 3–5–2 formation. He likes his team to keep possession with short passes, patiently waiting to strike, and encourages his central defenders to draw opponents out of position to join attacks.

YEARS AS HEAD COACH: 10

FIRST CLUB: LAZIO

CLUBS MANAGED	GAMES	LEAGUE TITLES
3	468	1
WINS	**DRAW**	**LOSSES**
275	86	107
CHAMPIONS LEAGUE TROPHIES	**EUROPA LEAGUE TROPHIES**	**OTHER TROPHIES***
0	0	8

*Excludes Super Cups

MAJOR CLUB HONORS

- Serie A: 2024
- UEFA Champions League: runner-up 2023, runner-up 2025
- Coppa Italia: 2019 (Lazio), 2022, 2023

DIEGO SIMEONE

NATIONALITY
Argentina

CURRENT CLUB
Atlético Madrid

Diego Simeone likes to use a formation which is almost a 4–2–2–2 unit, with wide midfielders playing between the two central ones and the strikers. Strong defensively, his teams are great at defending set pieces and dangerous in attack.

YEARS AS HEAD COACH: 18

FIRST CLUB: RACING CLUB

CLUBS MANAGED	GAMES	LEAGUE TITLES
7	941	4
WINS	**DRAW**	**LOSSES**
531	215	195
CHAMPIONS LEAGUE TROPHIES	**EUROPA LEAGUE TROPHIES**	**OTHER TROPHIES***
0	2	4

*Excludes Super Cups

MAJOR CLUB HONORS
- UEFA Champions League: runner-up 2014, 2016
- UEFA Europa League: 2012, 2018
- UEFA Super Cup: 2012, 2018
- La Liga: 2014, 2021
- Copa del Rey: 2013
- Primera División Apertura 2006 (Estudiantes)
- Primera División Clausura 2008 (Racing Club)

ARNE SLOT

NATIONALITY
Netherlands

CURRENT CLUB
Liverpool

Arne Slot is an astute and innovative coach. He has a reputation for developing young players and playing attractive, attacking soccer in a 4–3–3 formation. He sometimes operates a 4–2–3–1 lineup, with two midfielders in front of the back four.

YEARS AS HEAD COACH: 9

FIRST CLUB: SC CAMBUUR

CLUBS MANAGED	GAMES	LEAGUE TITLES
4	298	2
WINS	**DRAW**	**LOSSES**
189	60	49
CHAMPIONS LEAGUE TROPHIES	**EUROPA LEAGUE TROPHIES**	**OTHER TROPHIES***
0	0	1

*Excludes Super Cups

MAJOR CLUB HONORS
- Premier League: 2025
- Eredivisie: 2023 (Feyenoord)
- KNVB Cup: 2024 (Feyenoord)
- UEFA Europa Conference: 2022 (Feyenoord)

NOTES